blue
rider
press

GAY MEN DON'T GET FAT

GAY MEN DON'T GET FAT

Simon Doonan

BLUE RIDER PRESS   A MEMBER OF PENGUIN GROUP (USA) INC.   NEW YORK

blue
rider
press

Published by the Penguin Group
Penguin Group (USA) Inc., 375 Hudson Street, New York, New York
10014, USA • Penguin Group (Canada), 90 Eglinton Avenue East, Suite 700,
Toronto, Ontario M4P 2Y3, Canada (a division of Pearson Penguin Canada
Inc.) • Penguin Books Ltd, 80 Strand, London WC2R 0RL, England • Penguin
Ireland, 25 St Stephen's Green, Dublin 2, Ireland (a division of Penguin
Books Ltd) • Penguin Group (Australia), 250 Camberwell Road, Camberwell,
Victoria 3124, Australia (a division of Pearson Australia Group Pty Ltd) •
Penguin Books India Pvt Ltd, 11 Community Centre, Panchsheel Park,
New Delhi–110 017, India • Penguin Group (NZ), 67 Apollo Drive, Rosedale,
North Shore 0632, New Zealand (a division of Pearson New Zealand Ltd) •
Penguin Books (South Africa) (Pty) Ltd, 24 Sturdee Avenue, Rosebank,
Johannesburg 2196, South Africa

Penguin Books Ltd, Registered Offices: 80 Strand, London WC2R 0RL, England

ISBN 978-0-399-15873-5

Printed in the United States of America
1   3   5   7   9   10   8   6   4   2

Book design by Stephanie Huntwork

While the author has made every effort to provide accurate telephone numbers and Internet
addresses at the time of publication, neither the publisher nor the author assumes any
responsibility for errors, or for changes that occur after publication. Further, the
publisher does not have any control over and does not assume any responsibility
for author or third-party websites or their content.

Penguin is committed to publishing works of quality and integrity.
In that spirit, we are proud to offer this book to our readers;
however, the story, the experiences, and the words
are the author's alone.

*I dedicate this book to the straight women of the world,
whose lives seem insanely more complicated than my own
and whose shoes must surely hurt like hell.*

I feel your pain, girls!

Contents

GAY MEN DON'T GET FAT

SCREAMING
MIMIS

Suddenly last summer, I walked into a dusty shop on Capri and stumbled upon a cache of life-enhancing garments. They were nifty. They were sportif. They were also fabulously floral.

If towns and cities have a sexual orientation, and naturally I believe that they do, then Naples is a big fetid hetero and Capri is a colorful, tidy and escapist homo. Leaving Naples and boating over to Capri is like whizzing off to visit a spiffy gay uncle after working all week in a shed repairing vacuum cleaners—or something equally horrible.

We gays love the Isle of Capri. It's colorful and tidy and escapist, three things which are right up our collective boulevard. Especially the escapist part. While straight people devote their waking hours to starting gruesome wars and building nasty, smelly factories, we poofters strive to make life jolly and cute, like a chic cinematic antidepressant. In this regard, Capri always delivers.

And then there's the Caprese *passegiata*. That's what the Italians call the nocturnal stroll where everyone hits the streets. This is the ultimate mash-up of gay and straight, studs and starlets, a utopian fashion show of Fellini-esque fierceness. All the handsome Italian lads look like soccer players or gigolos. All the pretty Italian girls get dressed up and teeter down the Caprese cobblestones in strappy Dolce & Gabbana showgirl shoes. Think Monica Vitti and Virna Lisi. Think Marcello Mastroianni. Think Anna Magnani!

Often the Italian lovelies are linked, arm in arm, with an ancient gay mentor or, better yet, a wrinkled, belligerent granny. A hot Italian girl feels safe and protected when she has her toothless granny on her arm. And let's not forget, a wrinkled granny also provides a very flattering adjacency. For the girl, not the granny.

Capri is a delirious visual feast, gay in the very truest sense of the word. It's never grim or mundane. When you ride the funicular up from the harbor, you never hear people complaining about the threat of terrorism or bitching about annoying office mates or talking about needing to buy more stool softener, the way you do on the subway in New York City. Everyone in Capri is happy and has nice skin and, thanks to the abundance of figs, nobody has that wan, constipated look which you see in more northern climes. That's two bowel-related references in one paragraph. For a straight bloke, this would be unusual. For a gay who is focused on maintaining a colorful, tidy and escapist worldview, it's about average.

So there I am in this little menswear shop where I stumble upon the Holy Grail, or the gay equivalent. On the floor is a large basket containing a stash of swim shorts. A simple boxer style, all in an assortment of flower prints. Not big, tropical, gaudy prints. More like the fabrics which your great-grandmother might have worn in the 1940s. (Unless she was a streetwalker or a showgirl, in which case she would probably have favored a cheap, shiny satin.) Nice Liberty of London–type flower prints. Pretty.

Let's pause for a moment while I elaborate on my relationship with all things flowery. If you Google-image my name, you will see that, whether pimping or posing, I am invariably stuffed into a flowery shirt of some description. It's my signature flourish.

In the early sixties, mod boys like Mick Jagger and Jeff Beck and Brian Jones wore preppy-style shirts, sewn up in girly, flowery fabrics. When Ray Davies was belting out his satirical piss-take hit "Dedicated Follower of Fashion," he always wore a flowery shirt.

CUT TO: 2012.

I have a closet packed with dozens of flowery shirts. And, I am happy to report, they have lost none of their resonance and sizzle. When I don a flowery shirt, I always feel that little surge of provocation and optimism which harks back to Twiggy and the Beatles and the birth of cool.

Back to Capri.

With great trepidation, I begin rummaging to check the sizes of those shorts. My pulse is escalating. I am trembling. The chances of any items in the basket fitting me, little me, are more than remote.

Though not technically a midget, I am definitely on the spectrum. When I met Dame Edna, she bent down and peered into my face. "Goodness me, you are a finely boned little thing, aren't you," she said with faux concern, adding, somewhat unnecessarily, "are you wearing children's clothes?"

Thanks, Dame Edna! It's not my fault, you know!

My pixie-sized frame is attributable to the fact that Betty

Doonan, God rest her nicotine-riddled soul, smoked like a maniac when she was up the duff. Back then, in the eighteenth century, cigarettes were thought to calm the nerves of an expectant mother: "Feeling a bit fretty? Go on, luv! Have another fag." I'm sure it looked and felt very Marlene Dietrich to be wreathed in smoke while patting the bump, but there were ramifications. After nine months of puffing, out popped little me. A waif. A gamine. A shrimp.

When I was growing up, the other kids—in sharp contrast to Betty, their mothers had somehow all managed to get through pregnancy without the 5,400 cigarettes (pack a day × 9 months) which my mother had smoked—used to call me Shorty or Short-arse. This did not bother me. Everybody got called something. Better to be called Shorty than Snot-face or Weasel. And better to be a compact little gerbil than some big lummox.

I still feel that way. There are many positive aspects to being a freakishly undersized adult. When I fly coach, I can stretch out and pretend to be in first. When the subway car is packed, there is always room for a little nugget. When I visit Japan, I am always happy because, even though the men are all taller than me, most of the women are shorter than me. I can tower over them and feel manly and butch and domineering. This is not the case in the United States. With their porno-heeled pumps and their protein-rich diets, the women of America always loom menacingly over me. As a result, I have developed an intense familiarity with the area below their boobs. I stare straight at it all day long. If I had X-ray eyes, I would be looking at the pancreas and gall bladder region. *Bon appétit!*

The only part of being a quasi-midget which works my

nerves—and it is a big part—is the fashion part. When I go shopping, I can rarely find anything in my size. I have tried searching for stuff in boys' departments, but after I browse around for a few minutes through the racks of tiny garments, people start to give me funny looks, and I always end up feeling like an old pervert. As much as the salespeople might try to be friendly, you can tell what they are thinking: Who's that old poof in the flowery shirt who just took all that OshKosh into the fitting room?

The experience in a grown-up store is no less harrowing. Every time I walk in the door the sales folk say, "All the small sizes are gone. If you had come a couple of hours ago . . ." I always feel as if a tour bus of pygmies just preceded me, snatching up all the teeny-tiny tops and mini-caftans.

So there I am, rummaging through this mound of flowery swim trunks, praying that they are not all XLs when—eureka!—much to my delight I discover a small and another and then another. The swimsuits are all *size small*! I cannot believe my luck. Clearly the pygmy cruise ship has not docked here in a while. And if Capri is on their itinerary, they are going to be very, very disappointed when they get here because, in a moment of rash insanity, I buy every single pair, ten in total. Take that, pygmies! Take that, all you swimwear manufacturers who have forced me to stand in line for the boys' department fitting rooms at Brooks Brothers, looking like Chester the Molester. Ha!

Before surrendering my credit card, I take the precaution of trying on a couple of pairs. The fit is sublime. Bespoke. Custom. An Italian small is a real small. It's not like a Midwestern small or a big-ass Old Navy small. These swim shorts are flowery and nifty and perfectly cut and utterly couture!

Upon returning home, I anxiously await an opportunity to team my new shorts with one of my existing shirts for a floral cabana explosion. Ere long it presents itself.

My Jonny* and I invariably spend our weekends enjoying the rustic glamour of Shelter Island. We while away the hours doing wholesome things like hiking, kayaking and paddleboarding. (Not to be confused with waterboarding.) Our healthy outdoorsy activities may come as something of a surprise. Lots of straight people think that we gays devote our leisure hours to all kinds of nasty, unnatural activities. They assume that we spend every Saturday night tormenting each other with whips and chains and hoists while wearing butt plugs and preposterous leather outfits. Give a gay a night off, these naysayers think, and everything will just devolve into a drug-addled Sodom and Glockamorrah.

The truth is that, regardless of whether they are gay or straight, some people are hideously sleazy and others are more interested in needle-pointing pictures of thatched cottages. Some people get their rocks off dialing hookers in latex nuns' costumes and huffing glue, and others enjoy a nice outdoor summer barbecue. Speaking of which . . .

One beachy Saturday, me and my Jonny are invited to a barbie at the house of an acquaintance, a hetero New York chick, divorced, two kids, nice hunky boyfriend. What to wear? You guessed it, a pair of my Caprese shorts—an orange-and-yellow daisy print, if I remember correctly—teamed with a Liberty print shirt. The garment in question has an art nouveau feel and is dripping with

---

*My Jonny = my husband. Jonathan Adler, potter, designer, and the love of my life for seventeen years.

lilies. Feeling the need for a little accessorization, I plonk a cowboy hat on my head. A dab of sunblock and squirt of tick repellant and off we skip to the barbecue.

Upon arrival I jump out of the car, proudly fluff my florals and assume an air of international savoir faire. After decades in retail, I have almost zero social anxiety. Hordes of strangers? Bring it on! I just treat everyone I meet as if I am about to sell him/her a man-bag/handbag.

As it turns out, we are the only gays in the village, i.e., the barbecue is all hetero. There we are, me in my florals and my Jonny in his nifty Italian soccer player sportif look, just hanging with a bunch of breeders. This is not uncomfortable or unusual. I spend most of my time around straight people, as do all gay people. Unless you sequester yourself in some bizarre homo ghetto, that is the very nature of being gay. It's sort of like being a redhead or being Jewish, but not as rare as being a gay Jewish redhead.

While the wives putz around the pool, trying to prevent the kids from drowning themselves, we men congregate around the buffet and booze table on the verandah.

In the absence of any scintillating fellow homos, I focus my attention on the guys. I feel like Margaret Mead, albeit a more colorful and less frowzy version.

The attendant straight guys all seem to know each other. There is much backslapping and goofy badinage. Relaxed and liquored up, they are starting to let loose. I survey them and begin to muse. How does this special group, hetero males, get to be the dominant force in our culture? Why do they get to drive the bus, while we gays, riding in the back, are so much more fabulous?

I begin watching, listening and cataloguing the astounding

array of differences between our tribe and theirs. Gay versus straight. It's on.

Let's start with our faces. Right off the bat I notice that Jonny and I are a completely different color from all the straight dudes. While we are lightly tanned—you might even call us beige!—these breeder geezers are all bright beet red. While we gays cower under our parasols and cowboy hats or slather on our lead-filled total sunblocks, these straight dudes cook their epidermi until it looks like beef jerky after Wendy Williams has been roasting it with her Cricket lighter. Whether waddling around a golf course or hauling endangered tuna out of the ocean, straight men are too full of *Braveheart* bravado to bother anointing themselves with creams or unguents. That's a gay thing.

And then there's the conversation, or lack thereof. We make a couple of attempts to join in but are quickly reminded that straight male conversation has a totally different and impenetrable rhythm from our normal gay banter.

Their verbal interaction is as alien to us as their skin-care oblivion. Straight conversation has no common denominators with gay conversation. None of the dudes mentions *American Idol* or *Chelsea Lately*. Nobody Gagas or Ke$has or Beyoncés or slags anyone off. And nobody shares a beauty tip.

Typical gay conversation:

First Gay: Have you seen this new chick on *The Real Housewives of New Jersey*? She's vulgar. Hard looking. Sex crazed.
Second Gay: Wow! For you it must be like looking into a mirror.
First Gay: Fuck you!

Second Gay: Here's a flyer for the Michael Bastian sample sale.

First Gay: J'adoring you!

Typical straight conversation:

First Straight: Gotta fly to Denver tomorrow.

Second Straight: Luvin' my new Harley. That's her sittin' out
in the driveway. Ain't she a beauty?

Third Straight: Took me two hours to get here from
Westhampton. Kids are crying in the back . . .

First Straight: Fresno the week after.

Second Straight: It does eighty-five m.p.h. A total fuckin'
chick magnet.

Third Straight: Belch!

While the average gay conversation is interactive and riddled
with cheeky inquiries and wicked ripostes, the equivalent straight
conversation consists of a series of tedious, disconnected chest-
beating declamations.

And then there are the fashion choices.

Unsurprisingly, more than a few of the dudes are wearing
Tommy Bahama shirts. For a gay, these resorty garments are the
ne plus ultra of naff straight attire.* We gays would literally pull
out a crucifix if we saw one. I myself often have nightmares about

---

*For a fulsome explanation, see the chapter titled "The Most
Important Word in the History of Style."

being trapped in Margaritaville listening to Jimmy Buffett and wearing one of these beer-gut-disguising bought-it-at-the-airport hetero man-blouses. I wake up sweating and wishing I was dead.

"Nice shirt," says one of the dudes.

"Great cabana outfit!" says another.

My blood runs cold. *They think we are dressed alike!*

From the average straight dude's un-nuanced, uneducated point of view, there is no difference between my florals and his splashy Tommy Bahama muumuu. I cannot believe it: my sartorial choices have been blithely lumped in with the trappings of Bahamaville.

Tommy B. is not the only designer in the house. Many of the guys have opted for supersize versions of their kids' clothes: Billabong board shorts, oversize Quicksilver tees and hoodies and the like. As a result they look like freakishly hefty toddlers on steroids.

Which brings us to the stocky, chunky, burly, husky elephant in the room: straight men do get fat. Boy, do they get fat.

They are so rotund, if they rolled on top of me, I would be transformed into a floral place mat. It's hard to imagine how the wives copulate with them without getting their ribs broken. Maybe Shorty gets on top?

They are so chunky that, even above the din of conversation, I can hear the reclaimed floorboards groaning under their weight.

They are so bloody enormous that, if they all jumped in the pool, they would displace all the water à la Orca or Shamu!

It's not hard to see how they keep their ample figures. These dudes are literally eating their faces off. The main meal has not even been served yet and they are on a major munchathon! Handfuls of cashews, cheeses, bologna, pâte, and Spam are being hurled down their throats with such gusto that I station myself on permanent standby to perform the Heimlich maneuver.

Suddenly the hostess plonks a bucket of guacamole on the table and the frenzy goes into overdrive. It is as if she has fired a starting pistol. Still carrying on their "conversations," all the dudes storm the guac, double, triple and quadruple dipping their chips into the sloppy green oily mush. Mind if I throw up?

Restraining myself from shrieking, "Stop it, girls! Just stop it!" I make the effort to switch to analytical/caring/concerned mode.

Have these dudes any idea how much fat is entering their bodies? How will they offset this catastrophic intake of calories in the coming days and weeks? Are they planning on doing a cleanse? Who will look after their families when their clogged arteries catch up with them and they keel over? Isn't it always the way? The straight men bollocks everything up and then the rest of us are supposed to don a ruffled organdy apron and just pick up the pieces.

Assisting the ingestion of the guacamole are vast quantities of beer. After a couple of bottles the guys are all belching intermittently and obliviously. Soon they are farting, at which point me and my Jonny begin moving away, rapidly.

Observing this panorama of hearty, braying, unbridled piggishness is a mysterious-looking woman. She looks like a bustier version of Carine Roitfeld, the iconic former French *Vogue* editrix. Let's call her Solange.

Solange surveys the scene with a heavy-lidded gaze. When her eyes meet mine, they convey that languid, searing disdain which has made French women famous the world over.

And then she speaks: *"Quelle horreur!"* she says.

Solange, it turns out, was invited by an old pal under the pretext that there might be some nice straight men. So far, no potential dates had manifested themselves. After declaring loudly that she now wished she had been born a lesbian—this caught the attention of some of the dudes—Solange rummages in her fabulously beaten-up old Birkin bag, pulls out a cigarette and lights it.

Despite her monumental French bitchiness, I feel a certain strange, haunting solidarity with her. We chat. I admire her dress and correctly identify it as Azzedine Alaïa. She admires my outfit. *"Trés* sixties, *non?"*

We find a chic little spot away from the flatulent fellas and the screeching kids. We split a turkey burger. No bread. Just a soupçon of fromage.

After thoroughly cataloguing the sloppy antics of the straight men, we switch to listing the key components of our shared fabulousness. We are completely and utterly convinced of our own brilliance and taste. We are in love with our accessory choices. We are absolutely confident about our superb ability to deal with *"les hommes."* We are utterly sure of our sense of color, or "koolur," as Solange calls it. Most importantly, we are in awe of our shared ability to control our caloric intake. It's a veritable orgy of fag/frog smug bitchy self-congratulation. We just have so much in common.

As much as it sizzles and twirls and froths on the Isle of Capri, it is in the adjacent country, among the land of the frogs, that the gay sensibility finds its clearest and sharpest and bitchiest expression. As the sun sets, I have a deep and profound realization. Gay men are French women . . . with penises.

And at the same moment, at the far end of the lawn, a whole bunch of kids are shrieking and attempting to throttle each other. Suddenly two of them spot yours truly and start frantically waving. Then they begin charging toward me yelling, "Mimi! Mimi!"

I look behind me. There is nobody there.

They get about two yards away and screech to a dramatic halt. It is as if there is some invisible, impenetrable force field surrounding me and they have smacked right into it. Their faces fall. The little girl speaks.

"You're not our Mimi," she says in a very hurt and reproachful way, and they both turn around and stomp off.

Such is the nature of fashion and style, dear reader. When you make bold, creative gestures, you cannot expect that the entire world will read your cues with anything approaching accuracy. The straight dudes might think you are wearing Tommy B. and the brats may well mistake you for their grandmother. One person's gorgeous gay flourish is another person's hello mimi. One person's groovy, swinging sixties moment is another person's weekend in Margaritaville.

External validation?

When you adopt the role of style avatar, you must be prepared for any and all responses.

TART-TONGUED
and
BITCHY
and
WISE

Like many healthy inverts, I enjoy a bit of good smut, a dollop of trash and a soupçon of gossip. There is nothing we gays love more than reading about the misfortunes and skid marks of the straight world.

My introduction to the gutter press came early, courtesy of a rag named *The News of the World*, also known affectionately as "The News of the Screws."

Ah! *The News of the World*. In the long and tawdry history of tabloids, has there ever been a lower and more brain-corroding newspaper? How I loved it! Couldn't get enough. Ten years old and already I was focused on life's sordid underbelly. Most kids were not allowed to read this kind of gorgeous garbage. But I was lucky. Betty Doonan was an early and unwitting proponent of high/low culture. When purchasing the intelligent, mind-expanding newspapers every Sunday, she could not, try as she might, resist the siren call of *The News of the World* and its intoxicating headlines about naughty strippers, defrocked bishops and finagling politicians. Riddled with double entendres, these thigh-slapping gems were often from the WOMAN BATTERED TO DEATH IN FISH 'N' CHIPS SHOP school of copy writing.

Of all the lurid crap I salivated over in TNOTW, one story in particular stands out in my memory. Abandoning the usual relentlessly hetero focus, this journalistic masterpiece went in a completely different, taboo-busting, wig-flipping direction.

After hearing reports of various unsavory goings-on in the bushes of a large swath of North London parkland known as Hampstead Heath, an intrepid reporter decides to make a nocturnal visit. The hack finds, to his surprise, that the moonlit heath is far from deserted. There are men everywhere, walking, talking and occasionally sitting on branches in the trees. Are they ornithologists hoping to spot a wise old barn owl tearing a furry mouse to bits with murderous talons? Are they stargazing?

The reporter notes that these fellows are all dressed alike. They are all wearing—drumroll!—white turtleneck sweaters. He paints a ghostly picture of these white sweater–clad lost souls—are they a cult?—wafting and mincing through the misty glades and nooks of the heath in an endless, mysteriously choreographed dance.

The reporter bravely engages some of these outdoorsy fellows in conversation. Their responses are bitchy, tart-tongued and largely unprintable.

Having established contact, the reporter now begins to openly deride these men. According to him, they are the lowest of the low. Unsavory freaks. The scum of the earth. They should be put on an island and left to get on with it.

What, precisely, is *IT*? Inquiring minds want to know.

I read on.

"It" consists of a whole catalogue of blush-making atrocities, including hand-holding and kissing, and then disappearing into the bushes to embark upon God knows what.

And finally, the big reveal: These men are—even bigger drum-roll than the one which preceded white turtleneck sweaters—*homosexuals*!

The writer babbles on for many paragraphs, elaborating on the toxic horror of this strange milieu, laced with more tart-tongued quotes. The dramatic dénouement of the article occurs when the police show up. The Hampstead homos alert each other by squealing, "Lilly Law! Lilly Law! Lilly's here!" while heading for cover in the bracken.

This story leaves me paralyzed with excitement. A feeling of recognition overwhelms me. There is no question in my mind that this is my future. These are my people. I am destined to become a bitchy, tart-tongued man who will spend his Saturday nights scrabbling about in the dark in a white turtleneck sweater with a bunch of co-perverts.

But was I saddened by this realization? Was I depressed? Hell no!

All I could think was "Sign me up!"

For me, this white-sweater moment was an orgasmic relief. Finally I had something to look forward to.

For emerging gays, this watershed I-am-one-of-them moment is fraught with trauma and conflict and much clutching of pearls. Realizing that you are one of *them* can be very scary, especially if you are part of a squishy, happy family milieu. If, like mine, your family is more Munster than Partridge, then it's a whole other story.

The truth of the matter, dear reader, is that the possibility of joining a group of marginalized poofters represented, for me, a colossal improvement in prospects. Up until this point—this Hampstead Heath white-sweater revelation—things in my life were looking bleak.

How bleak?

Hang on to your toupee, batten down the hatches, glue in your dentures, gird up your loins with bejeweled girders . . . and I'll give you a brief* autobiographical overview.

Betty and Terry, my parents, met in a soup kitchen at the end of the War. Two months later, they got married and went to a pub to celebrate. Every expense was spared.

They then moved into a two-room garret, sans kitchen and bathroom, where they produced me and my sister. When we were old enough, they dropped us off each day in a public orphanage. This unconventional child care was very *Little Dorrit*, and not in a chic *Masterpiece Theatre* kind of a way.

War rationing was still in effect. Despite the hardships, Betty and Terry managed to sustain a solid marriage, no mean feat considering that everything around them was totally bat-shit crazy. If something could go horribly wrong with our relatives, it already had.

Let's start with Terry's side of the family: My dad's father shot himself when my dad was young. This sent my granny into a bipolar spiral which culminated in a random let's-see-if-this-helps

---

*As Dorothy Parker so rightly said, "Brevity is the soul of lingerie." Having already penned two autobiographical masterpieces and had my life unfurled on a BBC 2 comedy series, I feel I have done enough damage.

lobotomy. After coming out of the loony bin, still-bonkers Granny arrived *chez nous*—we had vacated the garret in favor of a larger adjacent accommodation—when I was about five. She was accompanied by my schizophrenic uncle Ken. He was even more nuts than she was. Sweet old Ken should probably have had a lobotomy, but was coasting along instead on Thorazine and electric shock therapy.

The main leitmotifs on Betty Doonan's side of the family were religious mania and alcoholism. In the case of my uncle Dave, this also involved petty but extensive criminality: he was on the run from the law and the notorious Richardson Gang of South London. His surprise visits always added an almost glam frisson of transgression to our strange household.

Let's take this cheery family montage and juxtapose it against the backdrop of the gruesome events du jour: In the early sixties, the newspapers were dominated by, amongst other cheery news items, the Adolf Eichmann trial. The horrors of the Holocaust were, for the first time, being broadcast around the world. Jews had been the primary target, with Gypsies and gays added for garnish. The fun people. The stylish people.

My mum's friend Erika was an Auschwitz survivor and frequent visitor to our house.

"Be nice to her, for God's sake," Betty would say, propelling me and my sister into the living room to make conversation with her sad, deeply traumatized friend. "The Nazis put her whole bloody family up the chimney."

Despite having prevailed against the forces of evil, postwar England was not quite the haven of free tolerance which an emerging gay fashionista such as me might have hoped for. I had four thousand reasons to hide my gay secret, including the fact that being a poof was not only classified as a mental illness, it was also illegal. Waa—waaaaa!

Add to this surreal Mardi Gras the fact that I had just been branded an idiot after failing the notorious eleven-plus exam, and you have the makings of a completely grim future. As far as British society was concerned, I was a mentally ill, criminal retard. Best-case scenario, I would end up working in the local biscuit factory with intermittent visits to prison. A more likely outcome: Yes, that's me waving from the barred windows in the poofter wing of the local nuthouse. Bonjour!

In the meantime I had to pray that another swastika-wielding lunatic did not try to take over the world, slap a pink triangle on my blouse and put me up the chimney.

When, in 2011, Dan Savage started "It Gets Better," it took me months to get online and create a video simply because I had no idea where to begin. My life has gotten so much better with time that it was almost impossible to express it in words.

To put it simply, the white-sweater poofs in *The News of the World* were my ticket out of hell. The notion of wandering around Hampstead Heath with a bunch of bitchy, snarky, feminine men in white turtleneck sweaters seemed like a gorgeously glam arcadia when compared to the other scenarios on offer. At least I would have somewhere to go and someone to chat with. And, most important, something to wear.

Speaking of which: The *News of the Screws* article included some wild speculation about why this mysterious group of chums were each wearing the same white sweater. The straight dude writing the article came up with all kinds of idiotic theories as to why the offending folk might have chosen to attire themselves in this manner. For example: they wore white because they wanted to avoid getting hit by a car.

The most glaringly obvious answer to this riddle escaped this heterosexual doofus. But not moi.

Even barely pubescent, idiotic, mentally ill little Simon Doonan knew why these guys were wearing white sweaters.

Cult schmult!

They were wearing them because they were rocking the latest goddam fashion trend, fur chrissakes. A white turtleneck was the sweater du jour. Everyone knew that.

Sorry for getting so bitchy and tart-tongued about this, but nothing burns me up quite like a straight bloke missing the fashion forest for the trees. I guess, after almost sixty years of dealing with straight idiocy, I should be used to it by now. Somehow the shortcomings of straights—men in particular—continue to astound me.

When it comes to trend spotting, straight men are, and have always been, incapable of identifying a grunge revival, eyeballing a new silhouette or even nailing a culotte. Heterosexual males may have walked on the moon, split the atom, invented penicillin and all the rest of that worthy crap, but when it comes to highlighting the bag du jour or assessing the longevity of the latest eighties bubblegum redux, when it comes to something really meaningful, straight men are totally useless.

Why are we gays so magnificently and unquestionably superior when it comes to matters of La Mode? Why do we have our finger so unerringly on the fashion pulse, while straight men are so out of it that they will actually wear a mauve Members Only jacket without any shred of irony?

When it comes to sartorial stuff, gay men have a very distinct advantage over straight men. An obsession with surface and appearance, while gruesomely absent in the hetero male brain, is an integral part of the gay experience.

To be a gay male is to devote endless hours toward annotating and decoding the meaning and nuances of hair, facial expressions and, most important, clothing. Whenever a homo leaves the safety of his sandalwood-scented lair, he immediately sets about assessing and evaluating the sartorial implications, triumphs and blunders of all those he encounters.

What drives this compulsion to pull out a mental clipboard and begin checking boxes every time another human being wanders into view?

Secrecy and nuance and codified communications are part of our way of life. That is how we find kindred spirits in the sea of hetero-mediocrity known as humanity. We top many people's shit lists and we know it. The ability to decode those around us at great speed can mean the difference between an evening of fine dining and an evening at the emergency room.

Example 1: Is this neat-looking man in the navy suit a Mormon/ Scientologist (not so gay-friendly) or a flight attendant (insanely gay-friendly). Judging by those Gucci loafers and that vacant earring hole, I would say it's the latter.

Example 2: Is this dude in the black leather jacket a Kenneth Anger devotee or just an angry sonofabitch looking for a gay to pulverize? Judging by the oodles of Chrome Hearts bangles on his wrist and the Givenchy leopard pants, I would go with the former.

As outsiders, we are constantly looking for clues to better understand the "normal" straight world around us. We search for that revelatory little detail, that dead giveaway which reveals some otherwise hidden aspect of a stranger's narrative. This is why we gays have figured prominently in the espionage community. Please stop shrieking with incredulity. Not all gays are hairdressers, you know!

The ability of a homosexual to assess the identity and intentions of an adversary while concealing his own has catapulted many a Leslie or a Sebastian out of civvy street and into a tightly belted trench coat. Paging Guy Burgess! Paging Anthony Blunt!

We gays are driven to analyze the appearance of others in order to survive. Straight men, on the other hand, don't have to bother with any of this stuff. They have few natural predators. Life hands them a scepter and an orb. They eat and fart and procreate until they fall off their throne. After a quick reupholstery job (by a gay), the throne is then filled with a new straight butt.

While straight men have occupied themselves with the business of ruling the world, we gays have, over generations, continued to obsess about matters of appearance. We have honed and refined our style radar. We are the bloodhounds of fabulosity. Now, in the twenty-first century, we are so visually and stylistically evolved that we have basically become Frenchwomen with penises. It's just that simple. Scratch a frog and you'll find a fairy, and vice versa.

They are fashion know-it-alls, and so are we.

Simply put: the gays and the frogettes both live in an impenetrable bubble of smug, bitchy self-congratulation.

There is, however, one major difference between those French chicks and we poofters: In our case, these feelings of superiority are 100 percent justified. In the case of Frenchwomen, it is merely a delusion, yet one more manifestation of that legendary *folie de grandeur*. While we homos are all genuinely authoritative on matters of style, French broads only think they are.

It's not their fault. The cliché myth of French soigné has been foisted upon them for decades. For some bizarre reason, every Frenchwoman on earth is assumed to have mystical powers and treated as if she were Coco Chanel or Catherine Deneuve, or Simone de fucking Beauvoir. With all this deranged projection, it was inevitable that these Gitane-snorting *biches* would eventually start to believe their own press.

Now it's time to *arrêter!**

If you want the skinny on style, then ditch the deluded frogs and follow the gays. We, not the Françoises and Solanges, are the true oracles. We are the chosen people. We, and only we, know how to enhance your tawdry, lackluster lives.

The reason for this is simple: We gays are a bunch of severely unconventional biatches. We are charismatic deviants with an eccentric worldview. We are *special.*

The quirky nature of the gay experience gives us the piercing objectivity and the bold originality of the outsider. In this regard, bourgeois Frenchwomen cannot even begin to compete with us. While French broads flail around with their fossilized notions of

---

*Lest you mistake my liberal use of French expressions for pretentiousness, let me reassure you that I picked up the habit from watching Miss Piggy. Moi?

bon chic, bon genre, we gays are rocking the idiosyncratic irreverence which is the foundation of a fabulous life. We, and only we, possess the indiscreet charm of the anti-bourgeoisie.

Take that, Mireille Guiliano!

The primary goal of this book is to extract useful nuggets and nuances from my gay life and hurl them in your direction, often with tremendous force and gusto. I want to liberate the women of the world—and maybe the men too—from all those dreary heterosexual, preconceived ideas and show them, by example, how to live life with the fearless, stylish bravado of us homos. Whether you are straight, thin, fat, bi, trans or just plain Chaz Bono, you can only benefit from a heapin' helpin' of my gay panache.

The secondary goal of this book is to make you laugh—something po-faced, humor-impaired Frenchwomen are constitutionally incapable of doing—thereby helping you to lose weight. I have a theory that laughter burns calories, but I have yet to support it with any conclusive data. With that in mind, I ask you to please weigh yourself now, and then weigh yourself again when you have finished this book.

Merci buckets!

Postscript: Did I end up on Hammy Heath wearing a white turtleneck?

Gay lib arrived. Homosexuality was depathologized and decriminalized and I was never forced to sit in a tree at night, hoping Mr. Right would notice my white turtleneck and come tripping through the bluebells.

We gays relinquished our white turtlenecks back in the late

sixties, after which the trend lay dormant for a while. White turtlenecks were subsequently co-opted by the straights and went through what can only be described as some very unfortunate periods. Remember that horrible trend in the eighties when straight chicks wore a white turtleneck under a baggy, dropped-waist denim dress, accessorized with a black velvet headband?

Regarding *The News of the World*: Just as I was putting the final touches on this chapter, the phone-hacking scandal broke. After manufacturing scandals, this delicious rag found itself at the center of one. At the age of 168 years, the gossipy old whore was finally stuffed into her casket. I eagerly anticipate the same fate.

KE$HA
and the
PRISSY
QUEENS

I feel strongly that the word "prissy" has been given a bad rep. What's so wrong with making sure your arugula leaves are free of *E. coli*? Why not use so much Purel that you have to buy it by the vat at Costco and eventually cause a worldwide shortage? Why not dab on a little Tom Ford fragrance before hopping into bed? What is the problem with sticking a raspberry-colored gerbera daisy in a bud vase and integrating it into your tablescape, next to your bedscape?

Answer me that, all you slobettes!

Any guy, straight or gay, who has ever lived under the same roof as a chick knows the meaning of the word "slob": pots of cold cream with cigarette butts stubbed out in them; toilets blocked with cotton balls and worse; pillowcases smeared with mascara; drains blocked with wads of hair and discarded fake lashes; and mirrors and walls covered in obscene, rage-filled messages scrawled with Nars lipsticks. Is there anything messier than a heterosexual broad?

Think I'm exaggerating? Follow me. Let's take a Hitchcockian foray into the squalid lair of an average girl. This particular person is named Tanya.

Opening shot: The camera pans a downtown skyline. It could be Detroit. It could be Dallas. It could be lots of places. After viewing various chrome-and-glass Ayn Randian office buildings, we eventually come to rest on one particular apartment building. We move closer. There is an open window. A shade is half-drawn to keep out the midday sun. As if by magic, we glide seamlessly into the interior gloom, just like that moment at the beginning of *Psycho* when we come upon Janet Leigh lounging in her white brassiere after a clandestine lunchtime shag.

But this is different. This is not a rent-by-the-hour love hotel. It's Tanya's apartment, and instead of a graphic Hitchcock movie set, this mise-en-scène suggests that we have stumbled into an episode of *Hoarders*.

If a suicide bomber blew himself up in a Goodwill store, this is what it would look like. It's the kind of room the average homo walks into, screams, "Oh! My God! Your bedroom has been ransacked!" and falls to the floor in a quivering heap of shock and revulsion, shortly after which he expires from the trauma of it all.

But Tanya's room has not been ransacked.

Tanya's room always looks like this.

Why?

Because Tanya is female.

At this particular moment it is impossible to tell if Tanya is *chez elle*. She might well be lurking in that armchair checking her Twitter feed under that pile of stained and rumpled Anna Sui and Isabel Marant party dresses. More likely she is still in bed. She and her roommate, Harry—we'll get to him in a moment—

were out late at some fashion show after-party, where they drank vast quantities of free booze and entertained each other with poorly executed cartwheels all night, in imitation of Ke$ha, their idol du jour.

The bed, under the covers of which Tanya may or may not be sleeping, is piled high with undies, suggesting that many hundreds of Tracey Emins* are cohabiting. Hanging from every picture rail and doorframe are satiny evening gowns, splashy cotton summer frocks, floozy blouses, puffy coats and skinny pants. Every lamp is draped with colored scarves. Hooker shoes and logoed shoe boxes spew forth from under the bed. Mounds of gaudy purses line the walls, many still carrying their price tags.

Next stop: the bathroom. Every knob or hook is festooned with hand-washed brassieres, black thongs and panty hose, suggesting that, in addition to the Tracey Emins, a dozen or so busy strippers are also residing in this abode.

The bathroom's available horizontal surfaces are crammed with skin-care paraphernalia. There is no brand loyalty here. Every product from Avon to Crème de la Mer is represented. Mountains of half-used free samples gather dust.

In the words of my Jewish mother-in-law, the whole place is a total *shonda*!

Now let's check out the adjacent room.

Wow! *Quel contraste!*

While Tanya's domain looks as if a pillaging army of Huns

---

*Excuse the obscure art reference: Miss Emin once famously attempted to win the Turner Prize with her unmade, pantie-strewn bed.

has just occupied it in order to stage a transvestite slumber party, this room is the raging, screaming polar opposite. It is so insanely tidy that it looks to be totally uninhabited.

What kind of psychotic neat-freak lives here? The polished wood floor and spotless, matte-white walls recall a monastic cell. Nothing is out of place. The overall vibe is that of a fancy hotel. It screams "Harriet Craig!" which is a bit of a coincidence since this camera-ready showplace is occupied by a bloke called Harry, Tanya's roommate.

Harry is all about scapes. He has never met a scape he didn't love. It started with the manscaping of his body hair and has now extended from his private areas to his boudoir.

His bedscaping is flawlessly professional. The pillows are perfectly plumped. The duvet—with matching Euro shams—is folded back tightly, but remains unimaginably squishy. The bed skirt hangs with the precision of a couture gown. The starched sheets appear to have been ironed onto the bed.

Next to the bed is a meticulously arranged tablescape: a Jonathan Adler lamp, a stack of books, a water carafe and an alarm clock. There is also an Hermès ashtray which serves as a *vide-poche*.

For those of you who were picking your noses during French class, a *vide-poche* is a tray or shallow vessel into which a dandified male empties (*vider*: to empty) the contents of his pocket (*le poche*: the pocket). A typical pocketscape might include a watch, a few coins, some man-jewelry, a condom and a business card or two. It is currently empty, suggesting that Harry may well be out at work.

Et voilà! Vive la difference! Harry the prissy gay and Tanya the hetero slept-through-my-alarm hungover slob. Each is diametrically opposed to the other, each clings to the belief that his/her way of doing things is the right one.

Today I will settle this dispute by declaring Harry the winner.

Harry is right. Messy Tanya is wrong, horribly wrong.

Among her many defenses—"This is just who I am," "I am just doin' my own thing, man!"—is the accusation that Harry is prissy. Yes, she dares to play the prissy card.

For the Harrys of the world—and the Simon Doonans—this makes no sense. How can prissy be an accusation when prissy is so clearly the path of righteousness. Prissiness is next to godliness. We are prissy and proud. *Vive le priss!*

For most people on the planet, the word "prissy" has a very negative connotation, suggesting an irrationally obsessive, prudish personality. Needless to say, I disagree with this notion: To be prissy requires guts. To be prissy is to fearlessly confront a blocked toilet, dig a hole in the garden for a dead pet or remove a dingleberry from a live pet.

Prissy is good.

Prissy is the foundation of civilization.

As far as those dingleberries are concerned, I am, as my dog Liberace can attest, no slouch when it comes to removing them. Whenever I find myself near the ocean, I always make a point of dunking Liberace's furry torso and washing away any little dried currant-size bits of poop from his most private arena. I have, in fact, become quite skilled at routing them. No dingleberry can escape my detection. Just call me the Dingleberry Whisperer. My prissiness, rather than preventing me from undertaking this task, is entirely responsible for the evolution of my award-winning dingleberry-removal skills. Take that, Tanya!

Whether scaping my bathroom cabinet, or fragrancing my undies drawer with Sables by Annick Goutal, I see prissiness as a life-enhancing force. This is doubly true for you chicks. When it comes to the organization and maintenance of your personal style and your fashion closet, you need to get your priss on.

For the blinkered Tanyas of the world, any suggestion that there might be room for a little prissification in her life causes her hackles to rise: suddenly she is ten years old again and her over-bearing mother is whipping her with a wire hanger and accusing her of not respecting the beautiful things which Mommie has broken her back to provide. Well, guess what? Mommie Dearest was right. There is nothing great about hanging an organdy party dress on a wire hanger. No wire hangers! Ever!

I realize this is the second Joan Crawford reference within a very short period of time. Since the topic is filth versus tidiness, it really is surprising that there have not been more. Joan Crawford's commitment to prissiness, both on-screen and off, has endeared her to gay men for decades. We have always been delighted and surprised to discover that such a tidy straight woman ever existed.

The late Miss Crawford was, in many ways, the patron saint of gay prissiness. Her when-things-get-tough-just-start-vacuuming philosophy has helped many a gay through a dark hour.

The Academy Award–winning glamour-puss was not just prissy, she was baroquely, creatively and monumentally prissy. La Crawford always carried a box of Kleenex with her in case her pooches pooped on the floor. Furniture and lampshades were all saran-wrapped against grime. White plexi sheets were installed on every window ledge to catch the soot. There were more objects wrapped in plastic in Joan's apartment than in the average Gristedes meat counter. In her hilariously smarmy lifestyle guide entitled *My Way of Life*, Joan boasts that her gowns or blouses were never reinstalled in the closet until "mamacita" had checked them for maquillage and sweat stains.

A sick, twisted, obsessive-compulsive bitch?

Maybe she got a bit carried away, but let me ask you this: Wouldn't you rather come home to a tidy pad than your current shit hole? Wouldn't you rather glide into a movie-star boudoir than your current it-looks-like-somebody-died-in-here crash pad?

I realize that the straight women and girls of America are going to take a little persuading before they prissy up their lifestyles à la Joan, and à la we gays. I find that an acronym is often a great resistance breaker. With that in mind, here goes!

P-R-I-S-S-Y

P—is for Paranoia. If you think that's black mold on your white-patent Marc Jacobs trench coat, it probably is. A healthy trepidation about microbes, lice and the like is the key to a happy prissy lifestyle. Girls! When you purchase new underwear, always assume the worst and immerse it in boiling water for a few days before wearing.

R—is for Repetition and Regimentation. We gays simplify our style journey by finding a nifty uniform look and committing to it. When I come upon an Acne jean that I like—one which accentuates what's left of my ass—I buy six pairs and declare them my pant of the season. This makes for an organized, militaristic and efficient approach to personal style. In sharp contrast, the Tanyas of the world are on a permanent, psychotically random buying rampage. Every trend and every style on earth is addressed and represented in their out-of-control closets. Now that style can be purchased at rock-bottom prices from the H&M's of the world, this sitch is only getting worse. All the straight chicks I know have gone totally bat-shit and succumbed to this deranged inclination to overassort their closets into a bewildering schizo mash-up. As a result, bohemian gypsy skirts hang next to punk-rock pleather leggings. Japanese avant-garde humpbacked jackets rub shoulders with floaty Isadora Duncan muumuus. It is as if women are now on a quest to find themselves by purchasing every style identity in existence.

In Harry's closet we find the ideal balance of reliable basics and personal expression. Here's a row of fourteen white shirts. These usually last about a week. Harry the priss likes to change twice a day. Ditto his undies. He favors dark denim jeans and simple V-neck sweaters in various improbable shades, from teal to fuchsia. To avoid looking dreary and samey, Harry adds flair and flamboyance with groovy, oversize vintage eyewear, nifty sixties ties inherited from his grandpa, a series of spiffy chapeaux. A fetching well-scaped beard completes the look. (Note: Harry's approach also works fabulously for butch lesbians and transitioning F to M individuals.)

While I understand that women have much broader and far-reaching fashion expectations placed on them than the Harrys of the world, they could learn much from the tidy anal retention of his uniform approach. My intention is not to curb the flamboyance and creative expression in female fashion: I am merely trying to create a situation where rats are no longer nesting in your Louboutins.

Between the gay inclination toward military efficiency and the all-bets-are-off freaky scene found in Tanya's closet, there is surely a middle ground. Girls, the next time you see a cowl-neck or a skort which truly feels like YOU, then load up and become, for as long as you can stand it, the skort 'n' cowl girl.

I—The skort 'n' cowl gal brings us to Identity. In the old days, a broad had one purse and one wristwatch. These signature items formed the foundation of not just her look but also her identity. Here comes Marion. Which Marion? Oh! Her, with the pearls and puce croc handbag. *That* Marion!

We gays tend toward the Marion approach. One purse. One bangle. I myself am a one man-bag guy. As I write, my Goyard—it's a messenger-style bag with oversize monogram—is nestling at my feet. I have toted it about for the last five years. The large initials SD emblazoned on the side result in my being approached repeatedly by strangers and asked if "y'all are from South Dakota." No matter. I love it anyway. My man-bag has become part of my personal scape. I do not need more than one.

I am not suggesting that girls stop shopping. I am simply suggesting that if they kept that yellow Givenchy purse a bit longer than a millisecond, then they could actually become "the girl with the yellow Givenchy purse," as opposed to being just one more gal in a sea of interchangeable bag-crazed lunatics.

S—is for Sanitizing. Call me Lady Macbeth, but I feel there is no limit to how clean a person might be. Full disclosure: I was a compulsive hand-washer as a child. My psychotherapist attributes this to a symbolic effort to ward off contamination from the out-to-lunch psycho relatives surrounding me. Lobotomies aside, you have to admit that there is nothing more appealing than a well-groomed man with well-washed paws. When I hear people say they like raunchy armpits or smelly feet, I assume they are lying or trying to wind me up and test the limits of my prissiness.

S—is also for Sluicing. I am a big believer in washing clothes, as opposed to dry-cleaning, or, as in Tanya's case, doing neither.

Though unintimidated by Liberace's dingleberries, I simply cannot handle the aroma of stale sweat on a man's tailored garment. This stench takes me back to my youth and the appalling BO which would erupt when various relatives—no names mentioned, Grandpa—would remove their stinking jackets. This smell—think farm animals in rigor mortis—seems to epitomize the worst aspects of heterosexual belligerence. It says, "I'm a straight dude and therefore I can smell like a pig and get away with it."

News flash: dry-cleaning does not get rid of this horrid odor.

The solution is very simple. Grab the Woolite and hand wash your garments—inside out and with special attention to the armpits—in the bath. Then hang the suit to dry. If it shrinks a little, and dries a little creased up, then so much the better. The stiff era of cardboardy suits is long gone. A slightly wrinkled suit gives a chic, Japanese avant-garde je ne sais quoi.

Example: I own several velvet jackets by Thom Browne which

I wear with jeans for a sixties Carnaby Street moment. When the armpits become whiffy, I run the bath and grab the Woolite and woosh woosh woosh. Voilà! So much more effective than dry cleaning. The resulting worn-in look recalls the velvet jackets which are worn by, believe it or not, swarthy, superbutch Sardinian shepherds.

Note to Tanya: My unpatented sluicing method is not just for geezers. It also works beautifully on blouses and silk dresses.

Y—is for Ylang Ylang. Sloshing on fragrance like a street-walker is very hetero. The Tanyas of the world often leave the house smelling like an Algerian brothel. Not Harry the priss, or me. For us it is a deep and profound, almost religious experience. Why? Because we perform the Valentino ritual.

Valentino Garavani, the iconic designer, has given many luxurious and squishy gifts to the world. His greatest contribution might just be his unique method of applying cologne. It involves four steps. First, select your cologne. Second, stand back, aim the nozzle in the air at a forty-five-degree angle. Third: press the nozzle and hold it for three seconds, thereby creating a cloud of perfume. Fourth and final step: now walk quickly and quietly into the cloud and allow it to settle gently upon your facescape, your cowl and even your skort.

Et voilà! Prissy and perfumed.

Once you have found your inner priss, what next?

Toward the end of the last decade I wrote a style guide entitled *Eccentric Glamour*. The goal of this book was to steer girls away from dressing like porno sluts, and to encourage them to treat the adornment of their bodies as a creative exercise, an exercise in personal expression. Say no to ho . . . and yes to eccentric glamour.

Under the umbrella of eccentric glamour I offer three broad categories.

The Gypsy: think Florence Welch.

The Socialite: think everyone from Jackie Kennedy to Kelly Ripa and thence to Beyoncé.

The Existentialist: think Lady Gaga, Tilda Swinton and Daphne Guinness.

It's been four years—a billion light-years in today's demented blogging, blathering, twattering, style-obsessed universe—since I coughed up this theory of personal style, and yet I feel that the basic premise remains sound. Tanya? Are you listening?

Before you head off on another of your booze-fueled shopa-thons, you first need to figure out who you are. What is your style identity?

My guess: You are a Gypsy with an Existentialist rising. You are Talitha Getty with occasional bouts of Tilda Swinton.

And prissy Harry?

Like many gays, he is just a big ol' male socialite.

The
FAG
HAGONY
and the
ECSTASY

To be a young heterosexual woman today is to be subject to the most deranged expectations imaginable. It is no longer deemed acceptable for young ladies to just blunder and waddle, ducklike, into adulthood by trial and error. Today there are no more ducks. The twenty-first century is a cruel, swans-only kind of a place.

Every gal is expected to emerge, age twenty-one, waxed, Botoxed and red-carpet ready, with a rack like Scarlett Johansson, an ass like J.Lo, and a face like Kate Moss.

What's that noise? It's the sound of a million old-school feminists blowing their brains out.

We worked so hard to free women from the bonds of looksism, and now, despite our efforts, they have all turned into a bunch of shoe-collecting, cupcake-eating, uber-vain bimbos. We give up!

As much as I sympathize with these feminist sentiments, I think I would, if I were a girl, be more inclined to seek out solutions or rather, *the* solution.

Become a fag hag.

CUT TO: a hair salon on Robertson Boulevard, Los Angeles.

Tamara sits in the salon chair, wearing the menacing black ankle-boots of a hired assassin and not much else. She is blond and heavily maquillaged, has plumped-up lips, a spray tan and massive fake porno-hooters. Her celebrity look-alike is Heidi Montag, or any of those *Real Housewife* tarts.

A tattooed Asian girl is gluing mounds of horrible hair extensions onto Tamara's scalp. On either side of Tamara sit two identical Heidi Montags, each with her attendant extension gluer. If you flew in from Mars you would think this was some kind of strange Heidi Montag factory.

Once the extension-gluing process is complete, Tamara, with her thatch of newly acquired hair, teeters across the street to grab lunch. This consists of mercury-filled tuna sushi and a Red Bull, during the consumption of which Tamara's endlessly self-involved inner dialogue rages through her brain. Like many girls today, Tamara has lots of important decisions to make. The crisis du jour? Should she blow this week's salary on yet another pair of pornographically high Louboutin shoes or might it be better to use her hard-earned cash to freshen up her vagazzle? Decisions, decisions.

At the next table sits Viva. There is a strange force field around this gal. All eyes in the room dart intermittently in her direction. Viva is hard to miss. Viva is compelling and enigmatic and unique.

Viva wears a short velvet vintage cape. She bought it at the Rose Bowl flea market. Underneath is a pair of Carven shorts and an Alexander Wang T-shirt. Her bag? A bright green fluorescent Proenza Schouler satchel. On her tootsies? A pair of Christopher Kane shower shoes.

The door of the restaurant opens. In walk three young men, Cedric, Arthur and Christian.

Cedric looks as if he is on his way to an Adam Lambert lookalike competition. He has choppy, jet-black, chemically dependent hair and kohl-rimmed eyes.

Arthur is wearing a narrowly cut pale gray cotton suit and gives the impression of working at one of the trendier entertainment agencies.

Christian's bohemian look is best described as yoga-sportif.

"Thanks for showing up, you tardy bitches!" Viva says, in mock reproach.

With much laughter, badinage, divesting of man-bags and jangling of man-jewelry, the boys plonk themselves around Viva.

The racket has broken through Tamara's wall of self-involvement, and she finally notices Viva and her boys.

Spray-tanned Tamara stares at pale and interesting Viva uncomprehendingly. WTF? How did she come up with this fabulous look? And why is she hanging around with that gaggle of sissies? As Tamara watches the scene unfold, she starts to get that I-need-to-get-me-some-of-that feeling. No, it's not Viva's satchel she wants or her shower shoes. It's the claque, the gang, the velvet entourage.

Viva is a new version of an age-old phenomenon: the fag hag.

Cedric and Arthur and Christian constitute Viva's family, a bevy of neat and tidy telegenic gays fluttering attentively around a stylish diva. They are Team Viva. They are the crew.

Tamara resolves to get herself a bevy of poofters. Up to now she has been doing it all herself. The result? She looks just like every other blow-up doll in West Hollywood. Today Tamara has seen the light: in order to achieve a level of creative originality, a hag needs fags, lots of them.

The fag-hag scenario shows no signs of endangerment. Au contraire! Every time I turn on the telly, I am confronted by some vivacious self-denying gay or other orbiting round a needy but fabulous trollop. It has become an entertainment industry cliché. From *Sex and the City* to *Coronation Street* to *The Hills*, representations of the fag hag and her attendant gay besties are ubiquitous and becoming more so.

Why fag hags? Why now, more than ever?

What is this strange contract between the fag and the hag? Why is it, both on-screen and off, on the rise? I cannot believe this important issue has not received an in-depth exploration on *60 Minutes*. In the absence of a Lesley Stahl probe, permit me to make an inquiry of my own.

Let's start with the fag hag. What motivates a Viva or a Tamara to acquire a flock of garrulous homos? Why is an adoring mo such an indispensible crutch for any twenty-first-century gal?

The answer is simple: a hag needs fags because being a girl today is becoming so bloody complicated that you need all the motherluvin' help you can get.

"Why is being a chick suddenly such a big deal?" I hear you implore.

"Where to begin?" I answer.

Younger! Thinner! Taller! Richer! Chicer! Groovier!

The pressure on gals today to optimize their assets and present a flawless red-carpet-ready façade to the world is out of control. Girls like Tamara are responding directly to this pressure. The Vivas of the world are creatively rebelling against it. Either way, they are both doing their best to contend with the overwhelming tsunami of demented why-don't-you-look-as-good-as-this imagery which bombards every woman on earth via every orifice.

In addition to contending with these insanely unachievable standards of beauty and glamour, gals today are also expected to be—*quelle horreur!—professionally successful!*

All the joyful laissez-faire of being a dumb broad has been yanked away and replaced by a crushing culture of overachievement. At the very least you better have, by age twenty-one, your own lifestyle brand, reality show, hedge fund and/or fashion line, plus a brood of three children with another on the way. So not only do you have to be Jessica Biel, you also have to be Sumner Redstone *and* that old broad who lived in a shoe.

Back in the day, we all understood that not *everyone* on the planet was destined to become Sharon Stone or even Jo Anne Worley. Not all of us had what it takes to "make it." Some people got lucky and hit the big time, but most folks just had regular lives, and they were often much happier for it.

Not today! Now, thanks to the Internet-fueled exhortations of our celebrity-driven culture, every gal feels compelled to compete with Angelina Jolie. Every slag wants to "live her dream."

I for one do not believe in dreams. I do not trust dreams. They are slippery and naughty. Dreams, let's face it, are just nightmares, but with better accessories and décor. Don't try to follow them, for they are a will-o'-the-wisp, luring you into a sulfurous, stinking bog of unrealistic expectations. Sorry to get all Edgar Allan Poe on your asses. I just hate to see you ruin a good pair of nylons.

This particular subject is, if you'll pardon the digression, one of my bêtes noires. I am constantly barraged with requests for help from young ladies who have been fed, and who have whole-heartedly subscribed to, the insane idea that everybody has to have "a dream." Everyone has to take the world by storm, shag it into submission and milk it dry.

When I tell them that they will only find happiness when they lower their expectations and start approaching life without all these ludicrous preconceived ideas, they look at me like I just fist-fucked Bambi.

They then execute a 180-degree turn on their Pierre Hardy platforms, pull out their bedazzled phones to check their Twitter— "I have seventeen followers! Yay, I'm Britney!"—and speed-dial their publicists to "check in."

To say that these goals are unrealistic is just a tidgy-widgy bit of an understatement. All these fame-whore dreams, combined with that delusional identification with celebrity, have transformed the groovy young chicks of today into dissatisfied, masochistic and horribly self-critical and self-involved lunatics.

Don't get me wrong. I'm not criticizing. I am, in fact, pro-foundly sympathetic to their plight. If I was forced to spend all day trying to morph myself into a hybrid of Gisele, Bill Gates and the Octomom, I would be a bit daffy too.

"Let's get back on topic!" I hear you scream.

No problem.

Given the monumental pressure to be fabulous, as outlined above, is it such a surprise that these hetero hags grab the nearest fag, put him in a headlock and drag him from pillar to vagazzle, from tattoo parlor to Rihanna concert? Hags need support. Hags need fags. Why?

We fags are a bottomless source of killer tips. We have finely tuned opinions about personal style, and are only too willing to machine-gun our hags with both solicited and unsolicited suggestions about frocks, hair and maquillage: "Don't leave the house this fall without a black body-stocking and a canary-yellow goat-fur chubby."

"If you are going to do both sets of fake lashes, then, for the love of Jesus, bag that burgundy lip liner."

"Are you a bohemian, or a faux-hemian? I think you need to think it through, before you spend fifteen hundred dollars on a fringed suede hippie purse."

We fags are also sympathetic. Having suffered the fraught complexities inherent in membership of an oft-criticized and marginalized group, gay men can empathize with psychological pain. There might be some eye rolling when the fag hag's back is turned, but when the chips are down, fags offer their straight female friends a sympathetic ear. They are also more than happy to discuss romantic problems in a commiserating, kaffeeklatch, ah-men-can't-live-with-'em-can't-live-without-'em kind of way. And fags are not competitive with women: the emotional support given by a fag is free of all that *Real Housewife* meshuggaas that often erupts between chicks.

Et voilà! Style advice plus psychological support: clearly, for the hag, it's a win-win proposition.

But what about the fag?

What motivates the homo to become lady-in-waiting to a stroppy, bossy, needy girl? What is the upside for Christian and Arthur and Cedric? How can it possibly benefit any dude to take on a chick like Tamara and spend all his waking energy with a petulant, overachieving Barbie who thinks owning lots of shoes makes her an interesting person? Why is the fag frittering away his pretty years as a member of any hag's unpaid retinue?

This is a harder question to answer.

In order to achieve a better understanding of the contract between fag and fag hag, I suggest we look at the history of this often bizarre and always noteworthy symbiosis. Fortunately for us all, historical precedents abound.

CUT TO: Eighteenth-century France.

The palace of Versailles was, in many ways, the gayest place on earth, an amusement park where ornamented fripperies and foofy self-indulgences reigned supreme. Packed as it was with *mouchoir*-wielding fags, it became ground zero for the fag hag.

The poofy tone at Versailles was set by a commoner fag hag whose name was Jeanne Poisson. When she became Louis XV's mistress, Miss Fish wisely rebranded as Madame de Pompadour. With her beauty and her passion for over-the-top glam décor and her gay following, La Pompadour was the original Kelly Wearstler.

Aiding and abetting Madame de P. was Louis XV's intermittently transvestite brother, who was known simply, and paradoxically, as Monsieur. Think of him as the original Rip Taylor. Despite winning battles and siring children, Monsieur is best remembered for planning szhooshy parties, wearing ladies' frocks, sticking ostrich feathers in his armor and indulging in what was known back then as "the Italian Vice."

Note: In French history gayness has, despite the shenanigans at Versailles, always been seen as some kind of *foreign* problem. At various times it was seen as "the English Disease" and, during Marie Antoinette's trial, it somehow became "the German Vice."

Anything but French, right? In the court of the Sun King it was known as "the Italian Vice," which, to my mind, sounds hotter and more appealing than the other two iterations.

Anyhoo, let's close our eyes and try to imagine the fabulousness of the Galerie des Glaces during one of Monsieur's foofy fetes. This gorgeous room is packed to the rafters with fags and fag hags. Imagine a cluster of courtier poofs flitting around some regal fag hag or other, Madame du Barry, Marie Antoinette or maybe good old Jean Fish, powdering and simultaneously pulling mice out of her giant wig, fluffing her twenty-foot-wide panier dresses, stuffing handfuls of potpourri down her cleavage and feeding her marzipan morsels while whispering salacious gossip in her ear.

Every ambitious woman in the French court had a fizzing cadre of helpful homos in her corner. If les garçons did a good job, fluffing and puffing their hag to perfection, then—*mon Dieu!*—she might win the lottery and become a favorite of the king. Bam! Instant job security for all concerned. By sticking close to their queen bee, the poofters were ensuring that they had a crust of bread to put in their mouths.

Et voilà! Reasons number one and two why a fag might endure the demands of a fag hag: career advancement and survival.

After the ravages and bloodletting of la Terreur, la fag hag went into hiding, and who can blame her. She hid in a cave, plotting her comeback. It took a couple of centuries for the fag hag to come out of seclusion and reclaim her cultural prominence. I consider myself fortunate to have been right there when it happened. I'm talking about the 1970s, or, as I like to call it, the golden age of the fag hag.

I know whereof I speak. I was fag to many a hag. Back then it was a different landscape. This was long before the Vivas and Tamaras, their velvet entourages and obsession with celebrities. In the seventies, there was more equality between the fag and the hag. We did not exist solely to prop up our hags. They were quite capable of dressing themselves. We were all in it together, unconventional outsiders hunkering down in the margins of society and having a total blast. Hags sought out fags, not because they needed an entourage, but because fags were, regardless of your background, a one-way ticket to freedom . . . and fun.

Becoming a glam fag hag was not about money or privilege. Au contraire. Any working-class gal was eligible. All she had to do was get a job in a fag-rich environment, be it a hair salon or a department store. She was then free to henna her hair, buy a few T.Rex albums and an electric-blue jumpsuit, and become a raging, screaming, eyebrow-plucking, feather-boa totin', fishnet-lovin', cocktail-quaffing, cigarette-holder-wieldin' fag hag.

Becoming a fag hag was a great way to beat the class system. If life handed you a second-class ticket and you had a deep-seated feeling that this was the wrong ticket and that you might be a lot more comfy if you were able to sneak into that tarted-up, squishy, velvet-draped first-class carriage, then all you had to do was become a fag hag. For a girl with disco delusions and a bit of imagination, becoming a fag hag was a way to enhance her life with a dollop of theatrical glamour.

Instead of becoming a put-upon secretary or a soccer mom, a gal could live a fantasy life, and twirl, metaphorically or literally, just like Diana Ross in *Mahogany*. Instead of dating some well-intentioned-but-boring-as-shit straight dude and spending your day imprisoned in a Dacron housedress and dreary, bone-colored low-heeled pumps, you could wear a vintage shrug made of jet-black, glazed cock feathers, with a spot-veiling fascinator covering your eyes, like Marlene Dietrich in *Shanghai Express*, and you could stare at the world with an amused, heavy-lidded, irony-drenched gaze.

Unlike the fag hags of today, with their heavy burden of physical and professional expectations, my fag hags only had two things to worry about: having fun and having fun.

Life as a seventies fag hag was spangled and sophisticated. A Shirley, a Sheila or a Sharon could jump on the sequined coattails of gay boys and we gay boys could take you to Puerto Rican tranny bars and cheesy dance clubs with light-up floors. Hanging out with us fun-loving, perfumed poofs was so much more appealing than dealing with smelly, beer-drinking straight blokes, the ones we gay boys often had our eyes on, the ones who just wanted to beat each other up and whose idea of a romantic night out was to shag Shirley, Sheila or Sharon up against a wall behind a pub.

We gays taught our gals how to ferret out fabulous historical tidbits and how to exhume eccentric personalities from the past. We all shared a passion for cool things and weird people, people like Yma Sumac and Yves Saint Laurent and Kiki de Montparnasse and the Marchesa Casati and Nancy Cunard, the rebel aristo who had a penchant for black men and wore hundreds of ivory bracelets, right up to her armpits.

By reading up on these taboo-busting style avatars, we all acquired a sense of drama and escapism: armed with our gay canon—see the chapter titled "The Bitter Tears of Jackie O"—we magically sidestepped the grimness of adult life. We found a way to feel very grown-up and stylish—the look of the average seventies fag hag and fag was often a pastiche of Hollywood grown-up glamour—while simultaneously prolonging the innocence of childhood dress-up.

The fag hags that I knew were all flashy dressers. Jerry Hall, Bianca Jagger, Tina Chow, Paloma Picasso, Loulou de la Falaise, Zandra Rhodes, Marisa Berenson, Veruschka, the Pointer Sisters, Angie Bowie, Amanda Lear: these were the idols and role models for my fag hags. It is possible that there were dowdy, frumpy fag hags with Iris Murdoch bowl haircuts and flannel skirts and thick underwear and crummy eyewear, but I seriously doubt it. To be a fag hag in seventies London, Paris or New York was to wear cat-eye glasses and be in a perpetual state of readiness to be discovered and shot for the next Roxy Music album cover. And to partaaay.

Studio 54 in New York City was the Wailing Wall for fag hags. Every one of them came to pay her respects and to show off her outfit. Fag hags in the seventies believed in the transformative power of a unique accessory: vintage marabou mules from Frederick's of Hollywood; a 1930s hatbox carried instead of a regular purse, a nightmare to get things in and out of but great for stashing a small bottle of hooch or a vial of . . .

And yes, some of them were, as per the stereotypical idea of a fag hag, on the chubby side. There was a gal called Leoni, a manicurist, who was the first person I knew to adopt a Louise Brooks/Anna Wintour hairdo. She enrobed her lumpy physique in forgiving men's silk pajamas. Very Claudette Colbert. Her accessories? Vintage suede stilettos and Chanel pearls.

Danielle, another hefty hag, distracted the eye from her ample physique by wearing exotic couture. She owned an entire outfit—complete with turban and peacock feathers—by Paul Poiret. For day wear she worked a Carmen/YSL/cigarette-girl look with forgiving but tempestuous off-the-shoulder blouses and red tiered taffeta skirts and fans.

Let's pause for a moment to reflect upon the plight of the chubby woman *en général.*

I am something of a chubby chaser, but not in an unsavory way. My undersize shopping struggles—for the record, my passport says that I am five feet four and a half inches tall—have given me a genuine empathy with fat girls. Yo, chubbies! I feel your pain! I can imagine how frustrating and disheartening it must be for you hefty chicks to schlep your big butts through snooty fashion stores, past racks of size zeros.

My sense of solidarity with big gals is very genuine. I love to be the wind beneath their wings. I have often fantasized about designing an inspiring, flamboyant and fabulous fashion collection for eccentric and intrepid plus-sizers. I hate to see a depressed fat girl hiding her light under a bushel in a gray or beige muumuu, thereby resembling a pup tent or a cinder-block wall. Much better to wear sequins and feathers and flowers . . . which brings us back, once more, to my fierce and fabulous fag hags.

When she roamed the seventies landscape, the fag hag was more than just a fashion poseur: she was a formidable force, a veritable circus act, especially after a few drinks. My fag hags lived for champagne and cocktails. Don't judge them. You would rely on the tranquilizing effects of alcohol too if you were young and excitable and libidinous and had to continually sublimate your sexual feelings for your constant and indifferent gay male companions.

Every fag hag had a special, signature beverage, usually something lurid hued and foul tasting, like parfait d'amour and crème de menthe. If, after a few drinks, a fag hag heard another fag hag ordering her signature drink, she would get irate: "Why do you have to order *my* drink? Don't take this the wrong way, but you seem more of a keg person! You butch slag!"

I look back fondly at the rabid anticonformist sensibility exhibited by these fag hags of yore. My hope is that by recounting their shenanigans, I will inspire the women of today, who tend, if I may be so bold, to copy one another rather than look for nifty ways to differentiate themselves.

I acknowledge that, with regard to the fag hag of yore, I may well be looking back at the past through rose-tinted cat-eye glasses. Upon reflection I must admit that it wasn't all cocktails and cock feathers: Some gals became addicted to drugs. Several of my close pals actually lost their minds.

A high-strung gal named Ginger snapped one day and stuffed her ocelot coat in the oven. Then she turned the oven on. High. The smell was indescribable. The fur coat was destroyed but Ginger wasn't. She eventually recovered. My fag hags were, by and large, a resilient bunch.

Take Lou, for instance: She wore leopard trench coats like a 1950s stripper and modeled her look on the iconic dominatrix Bettie Page. One night, in the back of a London taxi, Lou vomited into her purse, which was a shame since it was a beautiful black-patent vintage number, but better than vomiting all over the floor of the cab. Lou was well aware that if you threw up in a London taxi, you were immediately driven to the taxi depot and forced to hose and clean the cab for hours, until no whiff or trace of vomit remained. Fag hags like Lou were good at weighing up their options. She chose to ruin her purse over hours of scrubbing.

Like many fag hags, Lou was an anything-for-a-laugh show-off and a daredevil and she loved a good practical joke. One night, after getting locked out of her flat in North London, she woke up a neighbor who she knew had a ladder. Batting her eyelashes, she demanded that he climb up into her flat and then open her front door from the inside. Seeing an opportunity for a good chuckle, Lou added an extra zing to the escapade by directing her Good Samaritan to climb into the wrong flat, thereby scaring the hell out of a sleeping senior citizen. This was deemed to be very funny. Lou lay on the sidewalk and laughed and laughed till she vomited.

Along with a fondness for practical jokes, Lou also had a talent for seduction. Some fag hags had a knack for getting gay boys to shag them. Lou was one such person. She once yanked the Y-fronts off a gay pal of mine, leaving big, passionate scratches down his back. When I saw these marks of *sauvagerie*, I nearly dropped my cigarette holder. Having never shagged a fag hag or a female of any description, I was gobsmacked. No amount of alcohol would have been enough to turn me straight. This probably puts me right at the far end of the straight–fag continuum.

Nevertheless, I had some odd experiences with amorous fag hags. There was a boring girl in a duffle coat called Brenda who used to pounce on me and tell me she was madly in love with me and that she was ready to leave her boyfriend. She was of a specific genre, a gal who, out of the blue, randomly fell in love with a gay man and pined for him and stalked him. I never thought of these girls as fag hags. I thought of them as idiots.

I found the situation with Brenda incomprehensible and sinister. Whenever she came barging into the flat where I was living, I would jump out the kitchen window and run off down the alleyway in my platforms and gray-flannel oxford bag trousers, leaving my roommates to console her. I used to hide in the nearby bicycle sheds for hours waiting for her to bugger off home. Looking back, I realize now the bicycle sheds were made of asbestos. If I ever develop some horrible lung disease, I shall hold Brenda personally responsible.

Other than a few lingering asbestos anxieties, I have no regrets about my relationships with these women. Fag hags only enhanced my life.

Which brings us back to the question du jour: Exactly what is it that fags get out of these relationships? While the benefits for the fag hag have been easy to catalogue, the upsides for we fags have, as demonstrated by my historical-but-inconclusive-yet-hopefully-diverting meanderings in this chapter, proven more elusive.

I would posit the following: I think we gays enjoy complicity with a fag hag because girls are freaky and feminine and so are we. All of us had mothers and all of us are drawn, mothlike, to the weird, strange, compelling and ultimately civilizing energy of *les femmes*. Broads are intuitive and make life interesting and quirky. As a gay you run the risk of being surrounded by gay men and gay men, en masse, can be, as much as it pains me to admit it, quite greige. Too much male energy, even of the limp-wristed variety, can be mind-numbingly boring, as anyone who has summered in the Fire Island Pines will attest. A sea of fags sans hag is a snore.

A vivacious creative chick, even a demanding careerist lunatic, can mix it up for us gays and alleviate the homo-homogeneity.

There goes one now, strutting past in her Paciotti ankle booties. Let's go buy her a crème de menthe.

Postscript: What, you are doubtless wondering, happened to all my old fag hags? The Lous and Danielles and Gingers?

Lots of them got married, or shacked up, and yes, they stopped taking the pill and turned on the plumbing and had kids. Yes, kids. Before you call child-protection services, stop and think about it: What could be more fun than having a fun-loving fag hag for a mother?

For some strange reason, many of my old fag hags moved to Florida.

Look at that overdressed old broad over there, strutting down Lincoln Road in leopard mules and Capri pants. She's probably taking that scrawny poodle to the groomer. I bet you anything her favorite Bowie album is *Hunky Dory*.

WORK
IT OUT,
SISTER

Drive? Cooperative spirit? Organizational skills? Shoulder pads? An abundance of thick hair? A reckless willingness to grant sexual favors to all and sundry in the stationery closet?

What are the key characteristics of an exemplary employee?

If I were the head of Human Resources at some big company— a bank, a hedge fund, a sausage factory or whatever—I would always privilege the résumés of two groups: gays and former child-pageant contestants. Let's start with the latter.

Whenever I watch a child beauty pageant—it happens more often than I care to admit—I am always impressed by the up-an'-at-'em spirit exhibited by those bejeweled munchkins. This can-do positivity, if retained into adulthood, will guarantee productivity in any workplace.

"Defending child pageants? What kind of gay madness is this?" I hear you shriek. Yes, I realize that my opinions on this subject are utterly unacceptable and wince-making to most sentient beings, and that my pro-child-pageant stance is not doing much for my perceived wholesomeness. However, please bear with me. Try to listen with an open mind as I describe the character traits which are fostered by these tantrum-riddled rituals.

First and foremost, child beauty pageants teach resilience. The teensy-weensy competitors learn how to lose, and not lose heart. In life, thou shalt not always take home the glitzy Mylar trophy. Thou shalt not always be adorned with the pink satin sash. Sometimes, sad but true, the pink spotlight points at someone else. This hard, character-building realization comes early to those on the pageant circuit.

Second, child beauty pageants teach cooperation and social skills. Contestants learn, at an early age, how to share their mascara, and yes, maybe even a squirt or two of hair spray. Those of us who were deprived of that early pageant camaraderie find it hard, nay impossible, to share even the most bargain-priced beauty products with others. Bitch, don't mess with my Oil of Olay!

Child pageants promote mental and physical health too. Okay, so maybe that's a bit of an exaggeration, but you have to admit, there is no way that sitting at home on the couch watching *Finding Nemo* for the five billionth time burns more candy calories than high-stepping the length of a jerry-built catwalk in the banquet suite of a Comfort Inn in suburban Kentucky while wearing a polyester ruffled flamenco frock.

In conclusion: A child-pageant childhood develops skills which are strong indicators for future professional success. This small community may not produce a ton of Nobel Prize winners, but neither is it producing toothless crack hos and glue huffers. If in doubt, please remember that Shirley Temple, the primordial muck from which all child pageant contestants subsequently emerged, lived to become a U.S. ambassador!

Full disclosure: My obsessive focus on child pageants is fueled by a neurotic but profound belief that I somehow missed out. After an episode of *Toddlers & Tiaras*, I invariably find myself contrasting the showbizzy lives of these tarted-up tots with my own bleak, postwar, scabby-kneed British childhood and musing about what might have been: Why didn't my mother have the presence of mind to teach *me* how to bat *my* lashes, gloss *my* lips and twirl a glittery baton?

How come nobody in our house figured out that all I ever wanted was to prance about in front of a cheering crowd, bathed in adoration and soft pink light? Where was my spray tan? If only the excruciating boredom of my rainy school holidays—running down to the corner shop to buy my mum a packet of cigs was the highlight of my day—had been punctuated and enlivened with tap-dancing lessons, teeth whitening, Terpsichore, tiaras and tulle! Why didn't anyone plonk me in a salon chair and devote the next three hours to fashioning my tresses into an orgy of tunnel curls and cascading fin de siècle ringlets? Why? Why? Why?

Child beauty pageants would have been a great way—nay, the *only* way!—to alleviate the brain-mangling tedium of my child-hood. They are, in both their preparation and execution, mag-nificently time-consuming. If only my burgeoning gay sensibility had been given this kind of outlet.

Let's not waste any more time wallowing in regret, and move on to an even more employable group than those pageant grads: I'm talking about the gays.

Just why are homos so exemplary in the workplace?

As long as your gay does not become a drug-addled circuit-party queen, you can always expect a very high level of professional competence. We gay men—and wee gay men like me—pride ourselves on our efficiency. We thrive on the positive feedback which comes with a job well done. At the risk of getting all Oprah on your asses, I must point out that this approval-seeking behavior dates back to childhood. Most gay men were disapproved of by their horrified/bewildered fathers: "Why in tarnation is that sissy son of mine indoors watching Doris Day movies instead of skeet shootin' with me and his banjo-pickin' toothless Mountain Dew–guzzlin' brothers?"

As a result of this daddy disconnect, we gay men spend the rest of our lives seeking a pat on the head from a father figure. Bingo! Exemplary, big-daddy-pleasing job performance is the happy result.

In addition to efficiency, you can also expect a can-do level of professional flexibility. Gay men are more than happy to undertake business trips to distasteful, remote locations. An overnighter in Fresno or Duluth, for the average queen, represents a chance for random encounters. There is nothing a big-city homo loves more than to explore the unsophisticated boonies and hit the local gay bars. The outcome is rarely positive: these forays usually result in an evening of unpunctuated tedium and/or a dose of crabs. Once in a while, this kind of intrepid exploration can instigate real drama. Mistake a biker bar for a gay leather bar and the evening will suddenly be electrified with excitement, missing wallets and missing front teeth being the most likely outcomes.

But for most gays, travel is a positive experience, especially if jet propulsion is involved. The gays are the last people on earth who have retained delusions of airport glamour. Schlumpy hetero folk, in sharp contrast, regard flying as a gruesomely quotidian experience, behaving and dressing accordingly. As a result, airports are full of lumpen straight people, lowering the tone for the rest of us. But plonk a gay in an airport and—bam!—it's a whole other story. On go the Prada Italian movie-star shades. The cheeks are sucked in—both sets—and the head is held at an imperious angle. No matter how lowly his function, the gay is able, with an armful of fashion magazines and a cashmere neck-pillow with matching throw, to delude himself into believing that he is a traveling VIP, thereby adding a je ne sais quoi to his travel experience, and to that of his fellow travelers.

And there's more . . .

Whether on the road or back in the office, you can always count on us gays to be pathologically tidy. We never save rubber bands and bits of string and boxes of old crap, and we are horrified by any kind of hoarding impulse. If obsessive-compulsive behaviors manifest themselves, they are much more likely to involve frenzied hand-sanitizing and purging. This is a good thing. Fastidiousness, tidying and a mania for deaccessioning old files and accounts will bring a sense of order to any work environment.

Caution: At some point, important stuff will inevitably be flung into the trash. I would advise you to keep any *Bourne Identity–*level vital docs out of gay reach.

Honesty compels me to admit that there are a couple more downsides to hiring a homo.

The average sissy is blissfully unmotivated to retain or use the real names of any of his colleagues. He is far too busy being fabulous to bother with such trivia. The result: your homo colleagues will call everyone in the office by an out-of-date woman's name. Which name? Take your pick: Mildred, Blanche, Doris.

In this regard the gays are very democratic. Everyone from the secretary to the big poo-bah will end up with the same moniker.

"Hey, Ethel! Is Lord King Ethel in his office?"

Another possibility: Your gay may refer to everyone as Taffy, as in Taffy Davenport, Divine's daughter in the John Waters movie *Female Trouble*. "Yo! Blond Taffy! Please tell redheaded Taffy that her cubicle does not need any more pictures of Enrique, even though he's hot."

I myself prefer to call everyone Mary.

Good evening, Mary! Hey, Mary, how's it hangin'?

For me, Mary is the great equalizer. Mary is a stud. Mary is a starlet. Mary is a CEO. Mary is a cleaning lady. Mary is Democratic or Republican; if I met George Bush I'd probably say something like "Oh, Mary! You really should have done more for the gays!"

The burgeoning trans movement with its endlessly confusing new categories has only increased my commitment to Mary. As gender fragments and deconstructs across the country, I find myself more reliant than ever on my old tried-and-true solution: when in doubt, just call everyone Mary. Mary, Mary quite contrary. If everyone is Mary, then everyone is equal and nobody is a second-class citizen.

If you happen to call a colleague Mary and that person responds by grabbing you by the throat and slamming you up against a wall, there is only one option open to you. You must yell: "Murray! I said *Murray*, not Mary! Please believe me . . . Murray? Is that you?"

One last downside: Gays will quit unless you hire more gays.

In this regard, we are like those horrible geese which fly into the engines of airplanes. We can survive on our own but we prefer to get flocked. This is why we poofters often choose to work in more archetypal gay professions.

What, fur chrissakes, makes a job gay, you are doubtless wondering.

Let's take an analytical look at the pansy professions and see if we are able to come up with any common denominators.

First, and most important, it should be noted that the cliché gay professions are all innately slenderizing. Interior decorators don't get fat because they are continually burning calories. When they aren't rushing in and out of the D. and D. building clutching heavy bags of fabric swatches, they are flying around their clients' apartments strewing decorative accessories and moving heavy escritoires.

The same is true of other poofy professions: If you don't believe me, try zipping around a hair salon or a florist shop for an afternoon with a pedometer strapped to your Lanvin sneaker and then get back to me. You will basically have run the New York City Marathon.

My vocation—I refer to my groundbreaking climb to the top of the cutthroat world of window dressing—is not only the gayest profession, it is also the most calorie annihilating. When every day consists of climbing ladders, ratting wigs, glue-gunning sequins, stapling dingle-ball fringe and schlepping mannequins, you need the constitution of a high-performance athlete, hopefully minus any steroid abuse. Suffice it to say, I have yet to meet a morbidly obese window dresser.

I have been a window dresser for forty years. Not many people can make that claim. Most people age out of the display profession and embrace more sensible, grown-up occupations. Some drop dead from the exhaustion of it all. Few last more than a decade or two.

What caused me to tenaciously clutch my glue gun and staple gun for such an inordinate amount of time? Many reasons.

First and foremost, it's FUN! Like the other archetypal gay professions, the window-dressing community is filled with eccentricity, laughter and naughtiness. The typical department store display studio is a magnet for some of the most affable, freaky and eccentric people on the planet. Nobody is too strange to become a window dresser.

As I think back over those four decades, a cavalcade of funsters and kooks appears in my mind's eye: Ann Chovey, the Pyramid Club drag queen who attended morning meetings wearing a Dusty Springfield wig; Merkin, the straight guy who slept in the display studio for years without anyone knowing; Dora, the single parent whose Hare Krishna mother sat all day among the props and mannequins tending Dora's gorgeous interracial child; Roderick, the dope fiend who would nod out while using the band saw, and so many more. Ah, memory lane!

The average window display studio is mercifully free of any inhibiting supervision. Nobody from Human Resources comes snooping around. As a result, every day of my display career was *Romper Room*. No gray cubicles for us. We were free to say and do un-p.c. things and to skip about doing imitations of Bananarama whenever we felt like it.

Despite the obvious magnificence of all these gay professions, it must be acknowledged that they are somewhat reviled. People generally look down on these gay, step 'n' fetchit, service-oriented career paths. When a fancy Southern pal announced his desire to learn hairdressing, his mother could barely contain her disdain.

"Y'all know Francine, ma hayadressah? Well, why do y'all think she's ma hayadressah? She's ma hayadressah cos she's just plain duuuuummmb!"

If parents are derisive about a career in hairdressing, imagine how they feel about window dressing. It is hard to conceive of what the overachieving, intellectually focused helicopter parents of today would do if little Max or Gus came home and declared his desire to become a display artist.

"Mommy. I want to dress windows at Barneys like Simon Doonan. Can I have a staple gun for Chanukah?"

(Sound of smashing glass as high-strung mother hurls herself through plateglass window after gulping down cyanide capsules.)

The fact is that most people have a homophobic uneasiness about the homo professions. Even some uptight gays: A window-dressing pal of mine began dating a nice young man who just happened to be in group therapy. When this person told his group that he had fallen for a window dresser, the entire bunch turned into Linda Blair. They tongue-lashed him and accused him of "selling himself short" and "dating down."

The general snootiness displayed toward the gay professions is highly illogical. If the most important goals in life are to be thin and have enough money to buy a new Friday-night party outfit, then the gay professions deliver every time. The gays with the cliché jobs are slender, creatively fulfilled, and have access to great discounts. Most have a decent cash flow. The hairdressers, in particular, are coining it.

As a result of all of the above, we gays in our cliché profession are *happy*.

Of course, there are some exceptions. The late great Alexander McQueen suffered psychological torment which drove him to suicide. However, much of his conflict, if I may be so bold as to speculate, resulted from a deep-seated ambivalence about the intrinsic gayness of his profession. For a lad raised in the deeply homophobic milieu of the East End, the dissonance between his creative self and what was deemed manly was irreconcilable. His fame and accomplishment only widened the painful fissure. RIP, Alexander. You were a supremely talented bloke.

How, you may well be wondering, did my own parents react to my screechingly nelly window dressing ascent? Good question.

Flashback.

The year is 1999. I arrive at my parents' retirement bungalow near Belfast. In my bag I have a videotape of me receiving my fancy, coveted, illustrious C.F.D.A. award. Over a cup of tea, I announce that I have booked a room with a VCR at a nearby hotel. We can then watch the footage of the awards ceremony. This, so I imagined, would be my big see-Mom-and-Dad-I-turned-out-okay-after-all moment.

Betty and Terry seem mildly nonplussed by this idea. They look at me as if I have suggested something vaguely pornographic. In their eyes, renting hotel rooms for daytime use is something you do when you wish to obtain incriminating photographic evidence to facilitate a divorce. Betty herself had been obliged to go through this sordid charade when she cut loose Terry's predecessor in the late 1940s.

We ensconce ourselves in the designated hotel room. With a flourish, I order room service, cue up the tape, hit Play and commence my scintillating commentary.

"There's me and Monsieur Saint Laurent . . . there's Yohji Yamamoto . . . he's one of those mysterious Japanese avant-garde designers."

As I regale my parents with random recollections of the evening, I am anxious to demonstrate to them that, not only have I not become a junkie, lost my marbles or taken to drink, I have actually become rather fabulous.

Sparkle, Neely, sparkle.

As my bubbly and vivacious commentary continues, I become aware of a weird noise. It sounds like a motorboat chugging across Belfast Lough.

Eyes riveted to the screen, my name-dropping commentary continues: "Weren't Bette Midler's boobs fabulous? How blond is Donatella Versace? Horrible shame about Gianni . . ."

The mysterious background noise continues. By the time we get to the bit where I am delivering my acceptance speech, the grinding racket has become a dull roar.

The tape ends. I peel my eyes from the screen and turn to face the two squishy armchairs which contain Betty and Terry Doonan, or rather, what's left of them.

The scene which meets my gaze is quite jarring. It looks like the aftermath of a lethal gas attack. Jonestown springs to mind.

My parents are both unconscious.

Their mouths are open. They are snoring contentedly.

I have bored them to death.

The moral of the story: Whatever you choose to do with your career, whether it's foofily gay or relentlessly and boringly straight, make sure *you* enjoy it. Because, at the end of the day, it's your gig and nobody else really gives a shit.

One final and somewhat random word of caution: If a dynamic, charismatic gay—or, for that matter, a former tiara-totin' toddler—leaves your place of work, then you can expect a period of loss and immense turmoil. Brace yourself for all the complexities of a power vacuum. Nobody reacts well to a power vacuum. Recent developments in the Middle East—Mubarak, bonjour!— have shown us how hard this can be. A power vacuum in the office is no less unsettling. Even a regular vacuum can be trying, especially if the bag bursts or the cord gets snarled around your office heels.

The
BITTER
TEARS
of
JACKIE O

The whole world seems to be run by aggressive interns. In every work situation, I am doomed to collaborate with some precocious Eve Harrington, thrusting her ambitions and her "talents" up my nostrils. We live in a time when the aspirations and desires of the young are coddled and fetishized to an insane degree. But not by me . . .

Here's why I snapped.

I was recently working with one of these desperately overachieving, psychotically ambitious young lasses on a graphic design project. I advised her that the general vibe of her layout—it was an advertising mailer—was too sleazy and needed a little more uptown finesse. "Less hoochie and more Jackie Kennedy" was how I put it. The response?

"Who is Jackie Kennedy?"

The adjacent gays—myself and two other graphic designers—all clutched our pacemakers and gasped with horror. Our intake of breath was so massive that we sucked all the oxygen out of the room. Every nano-molecule.

Within seconds, people around me began to asphyxiate and

cry for help. I smashed my man-purse against the window, hoping to break it and let in some much-needed CO_2. The paramedics arrived . . .

Okay. I'm exaggerating. But you get the picture. It was horrifying.

I turned to the young Jackie Kennedy denier and, channeling Miss Jean Brodie, berated her.

"If your creative frame of reference is so narrow that it does not include Jackie Kennedy, and her legendary, chic but uptight, posh-lady personal style, then it is safe to assume that it also does not include Serge Gainsbourg, blaxploitation movies, Clarice Cliff pottery, Mina, Madame Yevonde, Madame Grès, Françoise Hardy, the fetish photography of Elmer Batters, Rita Hayworth, Jeff Koons, the art of the Viennese Secession, Alber Elbaz, Irving Penn, Shirley Stoler, Leonora Carrington, Ava Gardner, Isadora Duncan, Damien Hirst, Bjørn Winblad, Carine Roitfeld, Wanda Jackson, Nosferatu, Joni, Martin Margiela, Liberty prints, Cristóbal Balenciaga, Alexander Girard, Noguchi, Rei Kawakubo, The Shangri-Las, Brigid Berlin's tittie paintings, Zandra Rhodes, Debussy, Dusty Springfield, Biba, Otto Dix, Big Mama Thornton, Bonnie Cashin, Carmen Miranda, Gilbert & George, Christian Lacroix sweetie, Bettie Page, George Platt Lynes, Jackie Mason, Robert Rauschenberg, Kate Bush, David Bowie, the sinister whimsy of Florine Stettheimer and"—huge gasp—"the brutalism of Edward Durrell Stone. In other words, my dear, your creative frame of reference does not exist."

I pulled up a chair next to her and tried, fairly unsuccessfully, to adopt a less disdainful tone.

"The good news is that it's not too late. The solution is within your grasp. In order to enrich your mind and develop a complex, multireferenced visual sensibility you need a vast infusion of szhoosh. You need to immerse yourself in *the gay canon*."

The gay canon?

Gay people are cultivated, nuanced, with a fabulous and indisputable grasp of aesthetics, style and design. Whether you are gay or straight, a familiarity with the miraculous gay canon is the key to creativity, joie de vivre and not being a giant bore.

If you are straight and considering a career in a groovy visual field, or any fucking field, do not even think about proceeding until you have gayed up your imagination with a glittering and enriching foray into this wonderland archive of style, culture and glamour. The gay canon is not simply full of gay things. The gay canon is a broad cultural smorgasbord which provides a quirky, thought-provoking aesthetic linchpin or reference point for every creative moment. It is a beyond-useful source of inspiration, especially for those overachieving, annoying little straight brats who think they know it all. The gay canon will give even the dreariest intern a semblance of savoir fucking faire.

For those of you working in a bank or a Hertz Rent-a-Car office, I say this: The gay canon will add a je ne sais quoi to the *je ne veux pas* of your otherwise mind-numbingly tedious lives. Your job may be dull but you don't need to be. Keep reading.

What follows will be familiar to many gays—I have added some obscure stuff so the poofters don't get bored—and wildly unfamiliar to many heterosexual readers.

Each name or title in the canon will be followed by a micro-Tweet, a Tweet so tantalizing that you will have no choice other than to hack and Google and truffle for more info.

Let us begin with the most significant component of the gay canon: cinema.

My top ten life-enhancingly fabulous films. They are not in any particular order, and I would never do anything as un-gay as alphabetizing them. They are listed as they popped into my head.

PARIS IS BURNING (1990—directed by Jennie Livingston) Quite possibly the best documentary ever made—yes, even more compelling than *Grey Gardens*—featuring the viper-tongued Pepper LaBeija, the queen of "the Egyptian Effect."

THE BOYS IN THE BAND (1970—directed by William Friedkin) Gay hissy fits and cashmere sweaters, from the director of *The Exorcist*. This movie is the birthplace of the bitchy zinger, as in "Who do you have to fuck to get a drink around here?"

X, Y AND ZEE (1972—directed by Brian G. Hutton) Sometimes films are so crappy that they become great. Liz Taylor plays ping-pong in trendy early seventies London. Think *Who's Afraid of Virginia Woolf?* but with Thea Porter caftans and rich-hippie headbands.

SOME LIKE IT HOT (1959—directed by Billy Wilder) Humanity and beauty and the great dénouement where a drag queen finally gets the love.

FASTER, PUSSYCAT! KILL! KILL! (1965—directed by Russ Meyer) Bitchy, cunty, psycho-killer go-go dancers on the loose. The most beautiful black-and-white movie ever made.

DOUBLE INDEMNITY (1944—directed by Billy Wilder) Barbara Stanwyck plays a psycho named Phyllis who wears an ankle bracelet and enjoys killing people. So dark nobody would have the guts to make it today.

FEMALE TROUBLE (1974—directed by John Waters) Skid marks and glamour, and a fashion model so style crazed that she shoots up liquid eyeliner.

ALL ABOUT EVE (1950—directed by Joseph L. Mankiewicz) Bette Davis eyes, and mouth, and the birth of Eve Harrington.

MOMMIE DEAREST (1981—directed by Frank Perry) Forget about an Oscar—Faye Dunaway should have won a Nobel Prize. Declaiming her way through every scene, she puts the limp, mumbling "realism" of today's actors to shame.

SHOWGIRLS (1995—directed by Paul Verhoeven) Backstabbing Vegas chippies trade barbs and manicures. Pure, unintentional, unadulterated camp.

MILDRED PIERCE (1945—directed by Michael Curtiz). Exquisite film noir lighting, and a bitch-slapping mother and daughter both schtupping Zachary Scott.

ROSEMARY'S BABY (1968—directed by Roman Polanski) Who knew Satanism could be so stylish, or so hilarious? Ruth Gordon's Oscar-winning turn as Minnie never fails to hit the spot.

MIDNIGHT COWBOY (1969—directed by John Schlesinger) The best movie *ever* about New York City, and the best party scene featuring homeless people, European royalty, dope fiends and hustlers.

Okay, pedants, I know that was thirteen, but there was no way I could leave out the last three.

Once you have watched these movies, you will be eligible to undertake more sophisticated fare. I am talking about the great Euro-fabulous directors, the top ten of which are listed on the next page. Most are gay, a couple are bisexual and one or two are actually—shock, horror!— straight. All have produced exquisite canon-worthy masterpieces. After each director I have noted, for your convenience, my two fave movies from the oeuvre.

DOUGLAS SIRK—*Imitation of Life* + *Written on the Wind*

FASSBINDER—*Veronika Voss* + *The Bitter Tears of Petra Von Kant*

PASOLINI—*Salò* + *Teorema* (FYI: Pasolini died when a hot trick jumped into his Alfa Romeo and mowed him down.)

VISCONTI—*The Damned* + *Death in Venice*

TONY RICHARDSON—*A Taste of Honey* + *The Loved One*

ANTONIONI—*L'eclisse* + *l'avventura*

JACQUES DEMY—*The Umbrellas of Cherbourg* + *Les Demoiselles de Rochefort*

FELLINI—*Satyricon* + *Juliet of the Spirits*

MICHAEL POWELL—*The Red Shoes* + *Black Narcissus*

JEAN LUC GODARD—*Le Mepris (Contempt)* + *Vivre sa vie*

JEAN COCTEAU—*Beauty and the Beast* + *Orpheus*

THE BEAUTIFUL BIBLIOTHÈQUE

The gay literary canon is every bit as vital to the cultivation of your mind as the movies. Oh, wait, no it's not. Books are much less important. Watching movies provides much more aesthetic stimulation than reading books, and is infinitely less challenging to your A.D.D. Nonetheless, it is, on many occasions, worth making the effort. Here are my top ten picks from my own gaybrary.

A TIME TO BE BORN by Dawn Powell. La Powell shows that vicious, narcissistic, social-climbing Manhattanites have been around for a while.

SCRUPLES by Judith Krantz. A fabulously crafted pulp homage to the worlds of fashion and retail. Favorite character: Comtesse Liliane du Verdulac. La Comtesse is so haughty, superior, bursting with Gallic pride and know-it-all Frenchy ways that she makes Mireille Guiliano look like Dora L'Exploratrice.

THE CUSTOM OF THE COUNTRY by Edith Wharton. Undine Spragg is the first Real Housewife of New York City. Who knew La Wharton could be funny?

VALLEY OF THE DOLLS by Jacqueline Susann. The main character, Neely O'Hara, is a lethal combo of Lindsay Lohan, Tara Reid and the late Amy Winehouse.

THE PICTURE OF DORIAN GRAY by Oscar Wilde. Decadence, drugs, delirium and damnation.

SHELLEY I and **SHELLEY II** by Shelley Winters. The autobios of the great Oscar winner steamrolling through the twentieth century. Note the copious references to food.

NANA by Émile Zola. Common chorus girls, pretentious artists, bitter lesbians and horny old aristocrats duking it out for a whiff of Nana's perfumed panties in late-nineteenth-century Paris.

THE PHILOSOPHY OF ANDY WARHOL by Andy Warhol. Quotable, bitchy, swishy and brilliant: "Everything is more glamorous when you do it in bed anyway. Even peeling potatoes."

THE GIRLS OF SLENDER MEANS by Muriel Spark. It's a *Lord of the Flies* for genteel office girls of varying shapes and sizes. Spoiler alert: the chubby one can't squeeze through the window of the burning building.

MY FACE FOR THE WORLD TO SEE by Liz Renay. An obscure but page-turningly gripping autobio by an endearing floozy.

LA MODE

Fashion occupies a vast tranche of the gay canon. Gays are genetically predisposed toward self-adornment, and rightly so. Always remember what Vivienne Westwood said: "People who wear impressive clothes have better lives."

Another quote, this time from Edina in *Absolutely Fabulous*: "I want names, sweetie! Names!" *Et voilà!*

AZZEDINE ALAÏA—The wicked genius from Tunis, single-handedly keeping the *craft* of fashion alive!

MARTIN MARGIELA—The Greta Garbo of La Mode: strange, remote and utterly brilliant.

BALENCIAGA—Cristóbal Balenciaga was a Basque Spaniard who was so skilled he could sew with either hand. How gay is that?

DRIES VAN NOTEN—Belgium is known for serial killers, chocolates, diamonds and the eclectic genius of Dries.

LANVIN—Mega-talent Alber Elbaz breaks the cliché that all designers are misogynist poofs. He's definitely a poof, but he celebrates women in every seam of his magnificent oeuvre.

MARC JACOBS—Out, proud, kilted, tatt'ed, talented and keeping

American fashion on the global map. We used to disco down at the Area Club in the early eighties. He is still the unpretentious dude that he was back then.

CÉLINE—Maison Céline, as designed by Phoebe Philo, is about subtlety and Katharine Hepburn–ish virago style. Great for a rich, tall, rangy lesbian.

ALEXANDER WANG—The genius Asian du jour. Back in the eighties, it was the Jews—Klein, Lauren, Kors, Karan. Now La Mode is having a Suzie Wong moment. They are all brilliant, but AW is out front at the time of this writing.

ISABEL TOLEDO—The most talented American female designer since Claire McCardell, and the creator of the Obama inauguration ensemble. Part of the Cuban connection, which also includes another genius, Narciso Rodriguez.

JOSEPH ALTUZARRA—fierce, young, gay, cute and talented. A name to watch.

STRANGE PEOPLE

This might just be the most important canon category. The gays have a nose for creative, rule-breaking, taboo-busting eccentrics. If there is an Isabella Blow or a Daphne Guinness in the house, we will find her, pick her up by her Verdura earrings and put her up where she belongs, which might be on a throne or on the kitchen counter. New names are added to this list of lovely lunatics every day. Boiling this down to ten names was torture.

ZIZI JEANMAIRE—The chicest lesbian of all time and a dab hand with an ostrich feather: YouTube *Mon Truc en Plumes*.

LA LUPE—Latin insanity and a tendency to fling all her accessories into the audience while screeching: a petulant Latin precursor to Nicki Minaj.

RUDOLF NUREYEV—Style, cheekbones, panache and bulging white tights.

DOVIMA—The first and only real supermodel, with the most demented eyebrows in the history of fashion. Also worth Googling: Jean Patchett and Dorian Leigh. These girls made Linda Evangelista possible.

DIANA VREELAND—Speaking of making things possible, DV once said, "Brigitte Bardot's lips made Mick Jagger's lips possible." She was the queen of the sweeping grand pronouncement, as in "Pink is the navy blue of India."

EDIE SEDGWICK—Drugs, miniskirts and fake lashes. The house model for the Warhol crowd, until she wasn't.

SIOUXSIE SIOUX—Something unusual: a pretty punk. See also Nina Hagen, Chrissie Hynde and Lene Lovich.

ANDRÉ LEON TALLY—A tour de force of majestic fashion inspiration, in a chrome-yellow, floor-length crocodile coat.

LANCE LOUD—The first reality-show star, circa 1971.

TINA CHOW—The chicest woman who every lived and the first person I ever saw milling about and chopping onions in a couture vintage gown.

MOMENTOUS MOVEMENTS

No stool softener or enema required. The gay canon offers a sizzling familiarity with any and all specific styles and aesthetic movements. Here are ten for you to memorize and differentiate.

ART NOUVEAU—You just dropped LSD and headed to the entrance of the Paris Métro.

ART DECO—You are Lucy Tantamount in Aldous Huxley's *Point Counter Point*. You are a 1920s hood ornament in a cloche hat and you love silver and eau de Nil and dove gray.

SKANK MOLECULAR—You wish you had been adopted by Charles and Ray Eames. Even your cat has black wire legs. Cinematic ref: *Mon Oncle* starring Jacques Tati.

HOLLYWOOD REGENCY—You are having a moment of exquisite sixties cinematic glamour with a top note of neoclassicism and a base note of mod.

DAVID HICKS—You will die if you do not have graphic geometric floor coverings in every room and luscious mantiques coming out of your ass. And to you, Harry, from the second chapter, please note that David Hicks invented the tablescape.

ORIENTALISM—You are wearing a caftan and lolling on an opium bed and repairing a Sozzani wall hanging that your pet leopard just chewed. The paintings of Alma-Tadema get you all moist and excited.

CRIB-TASTIC—You are a successful rap star, or a Russian oligarch, who is splurging his "hard-earned" millions on salt-water aquariums and gold faucets. Don't mock! Better to be nouveau riche than nouveau poor!

SHABBY GENTILITY—You are suffering from delusions of country house grandeur—muddy wellies under a carved Georgian hall table—and loving every minute of it.

RUSTIC MODERN—You are worshipping at the temple of Nakashima.

RICH HIPPIE—You are spending an inordinate amount of time lying on floor pillows and channeling Talitha Getty and Anita Pallenberg. Lay off the hash!

That was just the tip of the Anita Pallenberg. Don't let the listy specifics of this chapter fool you. The gay canon is by no means finite. (That is the kind of thing a dumb intern would think.) The magic of the gay canon is that it is infinite. Like Wikipedia and those porn sites where people keep posting more and more alarming images of their unsavory erotic lifestyles, the gay canon is a growing, showing, startling, ever-changing thing.

In the name of Jacqueline Kennedy or, better yet, Jackie Onassis, dive in and drink from this fierce and fabulous fountain of fantabulous faggotry.

HOKEY HOOKERS
and
GYPSY
TARTS

Designer clothes have become so insanely expensive that many women are popping a Xanax before cracking open their favorite fashion magazine. When I look at the prices—$2,500 for a Chanel this, $3,500 for a stretchy Givenchy that—I often collapse to the floor from the sheer sticker shock of it all. While I am lying there, semiconscious, I invariably find myself thinking about prostitution. The only way for you, the ordinary gay or gal in the street, to afford those Balenciaga handbags, Proenza Schouler satchels and Rick Owens leather shrugs is by resorting to the world's oldest profession.

This is a very tempting notion. Why give away what you can sell? Why not turn on the meter every time you open your legs? At least you will be able to afford a few of what Fergie from the Black Eyed Peas refers to as nice-ies and ice-ies.

However, before you hang out your hooker shingle, I would like to offer a few words of caution and advice.

Prostitution is simultaneously glorified and trivialized in contemporary culture. Hoochies and biatches and hos and pimps are part of the porno-chic trend which has turned everyone, even people like Betty White and Cloris Leachman, into booty-shakin' pole dancers. There is a real danger that young people today, gays and gals, might start to underestimate the complexities of trading sex for money. Hooking might buy you a few nifty designer treats, but collecting the dosh is far more meshuggeneh-making than you might imagine.

First and foremost, it needs to be emphasized that prostitution is horribly drafty. As a former Brit, I have a strong aversion to any kind of moving air, especially if it's cold. Air-conditioning? Vastly overrated. But let's not get sidetracked. The reality is that standing about on a chilly street corner wearing nothing but a wig and a pair of oversize hoop earrings is the easiest way to catch a nasty cold.

But there is more to it. Much more. So much more, in fact, that I think the best possible way for me to proceed is to tell you of my own personal experience as a prostitute. This autobiographical tell-all slice-of-life will, I hope, offer a more complete picture of what's involved. Learn from me, a reformed hooker.

How did I become a rent boy? Good question.

I know it's hard to imagine, but there was a time when we gays lived in the shadows. We were, to quote Oscar Wilde's boyfriend, Lord Alfred Douglas, "the love that dare not speak its name." Now times have changed and we are no longer the love that dare not speak its name; rather, we are the love that just won't shut the fuck up, as evidenced by the book which you are clutching in your hot little hands.

We homos are all up in your grille, 24/7. You cannot open a

mag or newspaper without reading something about gay marriage equality, or Don't Ask, Don't Tell, or about really heavy, important stuff, like Brad Goreski's split from Rachel Zoe. Simply put: we are culturally omnipresent.

This was not always the case.

Back when we were stuck in those creepy, shadowy margins of society, peeking out from behind our Karl Lagerfeld fans, we gays were not sure how we fit in. How to live? Who to be? And, most important of all, how to earn a living? As a result, it was not uncommon for the fags of yore to sell their bodies. A hustle here, and a hustle there.

There was certainly no shortage of repressed, frustrated closet cases who were quite prepared to open their handbags for a little human contact, a little slap and tickle. And there was no shortage of cheesy, craven, tacky, opportunistic, cash-crazed, lowlife twinkies who . . . I'm right here, Simon, I can hear you!

Manchester, England, 1973. It's my final year at college. Funds are running low. I bump into a fellow student at a church hall jumble sale. After a childish and embarrassing tug-of-war over a 1930s fox-fur scarf thingy with heads and paws dangling off it— Halloween was coming up and I thought I might slice the dead fox into a bikini and go as Raquel Welch from *One Million Years B.C.*—we call a truce and pop next door to a filthy tea shop to commiserate about our financial woes over a cup of greige tea and a slice of gypsy tart.

Gypsy tart, I should explain, was a truly appalling, now-defunct British dessert which was so revolting—the main ingredient was boiled, congealed tinned milk resembling pus—that even writing about it makes me feel vomitacious. It is hard to imagine how we ate it, but eat it we did. In his stunning autobiography, the fabulous Keith Richards bravely confronts the horrors of gypsy tart and attempts to describe the taste: "pie with some muck burned into it . . ."

Back to 1973.

During the consumption of this hideous concoction, my pal excitedly tells me that she has found a new source of income. She has started to make extra cash by flogging her jumble sale thrift finds to fancy London vintage emporiums such as Antiquarius on Kings Road and the uber-groovy Virginia Bates on Portland Road. (Still in business and now selling bias-cut thirties numbers and nifty Victorian capes to the likes of Kate Moss and Lily Allen.) Her new incarnation as a vintage picker explains the aggressive posture over the fox fur.

My pal also mentions, quite en passant, without batting so much as an eyelash, that she has figured out an additional way to take the financial pressure off: she now gives her landlord a monthly blow job in lieu of rent.

I was so stunned by this revelation that I choked on my gypsy tart.

At first my pal thought that I was shocked or embarrassed, and she got all huffy and remonstrated with me for being judgmental. Once I stopped coughing, I was able to reassure her that, far from feeling judgmental, I was, in fact, filled with admiration for her entrepreneurial zeal. I would have said, "You go, girl!" except for the fact that this convenient phrase did not exist back then. So I probably said something old-fashioned and clunky like "Goodness me! You certainly are a very enterprising young woman. Good luck with this exciting new direction which your life has taken!"

I was impressed. Very impressed. Very, very, almost irrationally impressed. My louche pal had, as you are about to see, unleashed something rather wicked within me.

The following evening, as if impelled by a supernatural force, I got all scrubbed and twinkied up and made my way in my platform shoes, vintage oxford bag trousers, and my copy of a Mr. Freedom satin jockey jacket to a working-class gay pub near the canal in the center of Manchester. This is where I often started my Saturday nights. A drink or two and then off to a chichi disco called Samantha's. On this occasion I stayed at the pub with a pal called Vinnie, and got thoroughly smashed. I had a plan.

Vinnie was a trainee hairdresser. He was very open about the fact that, as a younger twink, he had been "on the game." But Vinnie was now respectable and had put his tawdry past behind him, unless the rent was overdue, in which case he was anybody's or, as he preferred to say, "most people's."

Drunken escapades, if you can remember them at all, are recollected in the jerky handheld camera style of the early Andy Warhol movies. There are no gentle fades, just lots of abrupt cuts.

OPENING SCENE: Me and Vinnie are locked in an intense tête-à-tête as he schools me on how to play the role of rent boy. Apparently the key to being a prostitute is *flaunting* yourself. Flaunt! Flaunt! Flaunt! He tells me to unzip my jacket to the navel, wet my lips, open my mouth wide and, this is the most important part, bite the air in a tempestuous tigress-y fashion. "You are living for kicks! Yes, bite the air, like a dog catching flies. Bite! Bite ! Bite!"

I am not sure how this flaunting and biting is supposed to attract potential clients, but I do it anyway, knowing that Vinnie has more experience in these matters. I am the trusting ingénue.

Cut.

As per Vinnie's instructions, I now position myself near the jukebox and start biting the air like a wild gypsy. Like a gypsy tart, if you will.

Cut.

That's me, drunk and disheveled and biting the air, clambering into the front seat of a banged-up Ford Cortina with an older bloke. This not unattractive Charles Bronson type is concerned that I might spew my guts in his vehicle, thereby rendering it even more unsavory than it already is. I promise him that I will not defile his Fablon-covered dashboard. I have a smug, drunken expression on my face which says, "I will pay my rent this month and still have money for jumble sales and more slices of gypsy tart."

Cut.

Me taking hours to get my key in the door, the way drunks do, and still intermittently biting the air for good measure, just to keep the client happy. The Charles Bronson look-alike, who has a strong Northern accent, shouts, "What the fook is wrong with you? Stop twitching like that and get the fooking door open!" and wakes up the neighbors.

Cut.

Me and Charles Bronson are rolling amorously around the floor of my squalid student crash pad in our undies. We manage to set off a mousetrap. Fortunately, nobody is injured. More rolling. (When, forty years later, I heard Adele's hit "Rolling in the

Deep," I was probably the one person on earth who had a visual for the oblique lyrics.)

Cut.

Close-up on my face. I am no longer biting the air. My expression has changed. My eyes consist of two crosses and my mouth is a zigzag. It's a face that says, "I have done something stupid. I have broken one of Vinnie's cardinal rules."

Cut.

Me and Charles Bronson, still rolling around, but now attempting to agree upon a fee for my services. Every time I throw out a number he reminds me that I have yet to pay my cab fare. That's a surprise! Apparently that car, with the holes in the seats and the crocheted steering-wheel cover, is a taxi of some description, Charles Bronson being the chauffeur thereof.

The good news: He seems willing to play the role of john. I will make *some* money. It's just a question of how much. The bad news: He is an enthusiastic negotiator who is adamant that whatever he ends up paying me for "my services," this amount would be subject to the deduction of his fare. He is, he earnestly maintains, a businessman, "just like yourself," who desires to be compensated for his services and deserves equal respect.

More numbers are ping-ponged back and forth. More snuggling and rolling about. Some laughter. More haggling. Though not unpleasant, the whole experience was a bit like having a three-way with a calculator.

Much of the rest of the evening was a total blur. I do, however, remember one thing. The money. That measly fee.

Even back in the economically depressed early seventies it

seemed like a paltry amount. What was the un-princely sum which I was finally able to extort out of my customer over a cup of tea the next morning?

Three putrid quid.

Okay, so I'm not Paul Newman, but I'm not Marty Feldman either, God rest his soul. Three quid. I had spent more than that buying Vinnie cheap cider at the beginning of the evening!

There is something really gruesome about three pounds. Even now it makes me wince. Two might almost have been better. I distinctly remember lobbying for five pounds, having come down from fifty, but every time he brought up that niggling outstanding cab fare—snog, grope, snog, grope—I could feel any advantage slipping through my fingers, like the sands of time, or of Coney Island or just about anywhere.

So three quid it was.

In the cold light of the next day I realized that I just might just be the world's worst prostitute. I was tragic. No self-respecting pimp would ever have tolerated my bungling efforts. I was a shameful embarrassment to the world's oldest profession and all who sail in her.

Let this be a warning to all you fags and flibbertigibbets who are contemplating a life of sin in order to satisfy your fashion addictions.

Prostitution has many moving parts.

Prostitution requires a steely focus.

Keep your knickers on until you have the money in your pocket.

A professional prosti must take charge from the get-go and demand his/her shekels up front. Negotiating while in flagrante delicto is a huge screaming no-no for any tart, male or female or gypsy. It is impossible to come from a position of strength when you are giggling a great deal and no longer wearing your foundation garments.

A
DIVA
on the
VERGE

We gays adore a tragic woman. We worship a dipso diva. There is a force field around every pill-popping pop sensation which ignites our gay souls and draws us in. If you, dear reader, are currently having emotional problems, then I strongly suggest that you gather some gays to your bosom as soon as possible. They will offer you emotional support and possibly a glass of sherry. They will not mock you, at least not until you are out of earshot. And if you snap, they will glue-gun you back together. In this regard, gays are better than Prozac.

There was, for many years, a big photograph of Judy Garland by the late great William Claxton duct-taped to the wall of the Barneys display studio. In this compelling image, Liza's highly strung mother is caught backstage wrapped in a towel. Her face is a festival of anguish. One rigor mortis hand claws the air. The other clutches at a bottle of rubbing alcohol which has clearly just been torn from her grasp. Judy is having a preshow meltdown.

Next to this picture is another, taken five minutes later by the same photographer. There is Judy, dressed in a black-sequined number, standing confidently onstage and belting it out to what one can only imagine must have been a sea of frenzied, weeping and adoring homosexuals.

Needless to say, these images were, over the years, repeatedly defaced. Speech bubbles were added to Judy's mouth: *"L'chaim!"* "Bring me a chai latte!" etc., etc. Fictitious liquor labels were applied to the bottle of rubbing alcohol. Despite the graffiti, the picture endured, a metaphor for the agony and the ecstasy experienced by creative types like us.

The list of iconic tragic chicks who enjoy gay adulation is a long one. From Edie Sedgwick to Maria Callas to Anna Nicole Smith, we inverts have accumulated a cavalcade of tragic, tormented, drug-addled lovelies in our gay hall of fame.

There is no shortage of contemporary tragediennes in the making: Tara Reid, Courtney Love, and dear old Brit Brit are working hard to make sure that today's gays have their fair share of Judys.

Why is it so important to the gays?

There are several reasons. Firstly, we gays enjoy a tawdry public spectacle. The public humiliation of another person, especially somebody wearing top and bottom fake lashes, is always compelling entertainment. There is something mesmerizing, poignant and cathartic about watching a histrionic female fall apart while we attempt to keep it together.

On a less callous note, I feel that we gays genuinely sympathize with these larger-than-life representations of anguish and mental turmoil. We have all had our moments when we wanted to grab that bottle of rubbing alcohol. Judy guzzled it so that the rest of us could be free.

At the turn of the century, I got a unique peek at the greatest tragic gay icon of all time. Judy pales in comparison. I am talking about Marilyn.

When Christie's auction house announced the sale of Marilyn Monroe's personal estate, my interest was piqued. When they called me and offered me the opportunity to design the auction installation, I reached for the rubbing alcohol and began screaming at the top of my lungs.

I have always enjoyed watching Marilyn wiggling and whispering across the screen. I relate to her desire to self-educate. I identified with some of the grimmer aspects of her childhood. Like me, she had done her time in a public orphanage. Like me, she had a lobotomy in the family. The shadow of mental illness hung over her. I know the feeling. I always empathized with her ballsy struggle to replace dismal aspects of her past with a life of glamour.

I remember well the day when M.M. kicked the bucket. It was 1962. I was staying with my toothless, drunken grandfather in Northern Ireland.

Every time he came home from the pub, which was twice a day, he was in the habit of announcing his presence with the phrase, "Guess who's dead?" Without waiting for an answer, he would divulge the identity of whichever of his old pals had given up the ghost on this particular day. A few days later he would transform his collapsed old face by inserting his false teeth. He only wore them for funerals.

On this particular day the questions "Guess who's dead?" was followed by him plopping the Belfast paper on the kitchen table. MARILYN MONROE DEAD AT 36 screeched the headline. "Poor wee thing!" he said, in a rare burst of tenderness. Later he went back to the pub and got thoroughly obliterated. I would like to think this was in honor of the screen goddess, but since he did this every day, it is impossible to verify.

Little did I know, as I read the details of her untimely death, that I would be fondling her frocks before the century was done.

Upon her death, Marilyn's personal effects had been boxed up and placed in storage, and there they had remained for thirty-seven years. I was present in the Christie's offices the day they were unpacked.

Paging Tutankhamun!

Unpacking Marilyn's possessions was a surreal and extraordinary experience. I touched her Pucci blouses. I folded her black capri pants. I found myself holding crackly, dried-up old shopping bags—JAX of Beverly Hills—filled with stockings, slips and brassieres. I touched hairbrushes with blonde hairs in them. I sniffed the Mexican wrap sweater she wore in the famous beach photo shoot, and detected a whiff of perfume.

The process of cataloguing and displaying Marilyn's bits took months. During this time I learned some crazily illuminating stuff about the breathy blond bombshell. Brace yourself for some next-level revelations.

Right away, I discovered that Marilyn was shockingly and unimaginably slender. She was sort of like Kate Moss but fleshier on top. Didn't see that coming, did you?

When it came to finding mannequins to fit her dresses, I simply couldn't. M.M.'s drag was too small for the average window dummy. Smaller "petite" mannequins existed but I could not bring myself to place Marilyn's iconic garments on these perky fiberglass dollies. The frocks seemed too important and historic. For the public installation I decided to give them the Shroud of Turin treatment.

I laid the dresses in rows on top of angled panels—sort of like bodies after a plane crash—and accompanied them with a photo of M.M. herself in each frock. It worked. There was the black strappy gown she wore in Korea. And there, in the adjacent photo, was M.M. strutting about in front of the troops.

The only exception was the sparkly Jean Louis number Marilyn wore for the Kennedy happy-birthday chanson. For this dress, a custom Lucite mannequin was made.

Let's return for a moment to that revelation about Marilyn's size. Prepare to get extremely depressed.

When you look at Marilyn on-screen and—armed with the information I have just provided—you realize that the busty, ample gal brimming over Tony Curtis in *Some Like It Hot* is literally one-third *your* size, you have every right to become suicidal. If she looks like that—zaftig, almost chubby—what on earth would you look like under similar circumstances?

Conventional wisdom says that the camera adds five pounds. After my Marilyn experience, I would say it's more like five hundred pounds.

This schism, between what one thinks one actually looks like and what one looks like when one is represented on film or in a photograph, is a central issue for the women and gays of today. This is why we, the gays and the girls, make fat jokes all day long.

We live in an age where photo documentation is not just part of life, it *is* life. Any and all social gatherings are relentlessly filmed and YouTubed and snapped and Facebooked to the point where people do not even feel they exist unless somebody is lensing the moment.

This is all fine and dandy except for one thing: according to this photograph you now have more chins than the Peking phone book.

Why are we doing this to ourselves? Cameras are not our friends. Photographs are brutal and unkind. They ricochet images in which we look three times fatter than we thought we were. Back in Marilyn's day it was only movie stars whose lives were so ferociously documented. Now it is every gay and every girl on earth.

As a result we are all striving for a new level of thinness. Now we all desperately want to be camera-thin. This has forced girls and gays to adopt extreme measures. In every office across the country every gal and every gay has a bottle of an alarming bilge-colored beverage at hand.

"I'm on a cleanse" is the mantra du jour.

No gal will walk down the office hallway unless she is wearing skyscraper porno heels that attenuate her entire body into camera-readiness. We have all turned into a bunch of Marilyns.

This combo of heels and cleanses has had bizarre repercussions for all you girls. Yes, I am talking about those grim, black Darth Vader leg casts which you girls all seem to have adopted as your accessory du jour.

Every time I leave my house I encounter a glamorous chippie hobbling down the street with a broken foot encased in one of these massively unwieldy high-tech orthopedic gladiatorial thingys. I recently started to count them, and, at the time of writing, I am averaging five per day. Clearly those trendy starvation diets and juice cleanses are taking their toll. Cinematic perfection has a price. As bone density has plummeted, heels have risen. The lethal combo of fragile feet and outrageous Pierre Hardys, Alaïas and Louboutins has produced this catastrophic, futuristic plague. Where will it end?

It will end with us gays pushing all our girlfriends around in wheelchairs.

Before we move on to my next Marilyn revelation, and before anyone takes yet one more unflattering picture of your ass, let me offer you a couple of great posing tips. You cannot stop your drunken pals from taking your picture, but you can minimize the horror with a little fashion insider knowledge.

Tip 1: THURSDAY. Irving Penn, the greatest fashion photographer of all time, allegedly advised his models to say the word "Thursday" right before he snapped his camera. Thursday was his "cheese." "Thursday" creates a glamorous moue followed by a natural, subtle smile. If some crazy chick lurches toward you with an iPhone, say "Thursday" and hope for the best.

Tip 2: CHIN ON THE LEDGE. Kate Moss has been overheard repeating the phrase "chin on the ledge" while shooting. Kate's mantra is accompanied by a light neck stretch and a proffering toward the camera of her magnificent bone structure. Kate's tip will maximize what little neck you have and minimize your chins.

No offense!

And for my second Marilyn bet-you-didn't-see-that-coming revelation . . .

Marilyn Monroe was a huge movie star, but she owned diddly-squat. *She was not materialistic!*

Marilyn's estate was a bunch of poignant schlock. The auction raised more than thirteen million dollars, but not because of any intrinsic value in the numbered lots. There were no Renoirs or Picassos. Her knickknacks were pedestrian. Her cookware was greasy. Her spatulas were bent. Even her Golden Globe was broken.

The majority of her clothing showed surprising wear and tear. She had worn it all repeatedly and there just wasn't that much of it.

Her jewelry? With the exception of her DiMaggio wedding ring it was a bunch of paste danglers and costume crap.

Shoes? Yes, there were several pairs of black suede Ferragamo stilettos with worn heels. But Marilyn—brace yourself for another shocker—was more into books than shoes. Her poignant desire to cultivate her mind and give herself an education resulted in an extensive library of first editions. Take that, Carrie Bradshaw!

This stunning lack of materialism made me love and respect her more. What do you need in life other than a good book, a few capri pants and a cotton sundress or two?

Yes, there were a few fur coats. But compared to the gimme-gimme-gimme stars of today whose hangar-size closets are bursting with freebies, she was a total bread-and-water-eating, hair-shirt-wearing, self-denying nun.

Marilyn the enigma. Marilyn the sphinx. Marilyn the gay icon. Will she endure?

According to marketing folks at Christie's, the M.M. auction was timed to coincide with the turn of the century, after which it was anticipated that her popularity would begin a slow and natural decline. Stop screeching with horror and indignation and remember that exactly the same thing happened to those silent-movie stars, back in the day. In 1920 Mary Pickford—in many ways far more famous and well liked than Marilyn—could not leave her house without hordes of people yanking on her ringlets. Mary who? And when Rudolph Valentino died, there were riots and people killed themselves. Does anybody remember the old kohl-eyed poof now?

I recently rewatched *Some Like It Hot*. When Marilyn walks down the train platform—her luminescent beauty is showcased in a black tailored fur-trimmed coat with a feather-trimmed cloche hat, and she is clutching her little ukulele case—she is the hippest, most stylish chick in the universe. It's hard to imagine that the poofs and style addicts of the future will not get a chill when they encounter such loveliness.

MACA-ROONS *are* SO GAY!

Popular wisdom dictates that there are four food groups: meat, dairy, grains, and fruits and vegetables. I disagree. As far as I am concerned, there are only two food groups: gay food and straight food.

The use of the word "gay" is constantly evolving. Yes, it still means homosexual, but only sometimes. Unfortunately, "gay" has come to signify a whole bewildering passel of things, none of them particularly nice.

When I was a teeny, tiny, twinkle-toed toddler, "gay" meant "cheery and/or brightly colored," as in your granny's kitchen curtains, or a post-hysterectomy pick-me-up bouquet of mixed blooms. How gay!

Then, all of a sudden, the louche seventies arrived and the meaning got significantly edgier: instead of being used to describe the pretty, flowery dust-ruffle on Aunt Mitzi's bed skirt, "gay" now meant "takes it up the ass."

As we career into the second decade of the twenty-first century, "gay" has many, many, many meanings, including, but not limited to, "asshole."

This has happened because political correctness now forbids young people from using the old tried-and-true repertoire of horrible insults and slurs. In the absence of "cunt," "spick" and the n-word, "gay" has become the go-to slur for the hoodlums and hos of the world. And it has become quite popular. I hear young kids on the street in my neighborhood tossing "gay" at each other as if it was a beaten-up Blahnik missing a heel.

There is, you will be surprised to hear, a certain context where I find the gratuitous and frivolous use of the word "gay" to be justified and actually quite helpful.

I am talking about food.

Simply put: Straight foods are basic and uncontrived. Gay foods are fiddly and foofy.

Straight foods are dark of hue. Gay foods are brightly colored.

Straight foods are often protein rich. Gay foods are nice to look at, but may contain little or no protein. For example: lettuce. As Diana Vreeland once said, "Lettuce is divine, although I'm not sure it's really a food."

Sushi may well be the gayest food on earth. The design of the average *ikura gunkan maki* or *hirame nigiri* is, if you look at it objectively, really quite extraordinary. Sushi chefs are basically taking sloppy bits of fish and magically reworking them into exquisite bonbons. How gay, right?

Regarding fishy bonbons: I have it on good authority from a Japanese pal that sushi chef is a gay profession, sort of like the Jap version of hairdresser. My brother Hiro is, you know, a sushi chef. *Nudge, nudge. Wink, wink.* Whenever I go to a sushi bar, I keep this little factoid in mind. I always make a point of waving kittenishly at the sushi chef and making goo-goo eyes. I have yet to receive any kind of response or free sushi. I am starting to think that my pal may have set me up. If I am ever found dead in an alley, reeking of sake and smeared in wasabi, you will know the reason why.

Moving right along . . .

While sushi is swishy, Mexican food is unbelievably macho. As delicious as a burrito is, it is basically just a cross between a turd and a penis. And that delicious green and mudlike guacamole is, obviously, 100 percent heterosexual. There are, of course, a few notable exceptions. While a slab of boiled beef smothered in thick, dark brown mole is clearly hetero, an exploding tostada with mountains of frilly lettuce on top is the ne plus ultra of supergay, and superdelicious. *¡Qué rico!*

Italian food is unarguably, unrelentingly Tony Soprano straight. Some of it is even Big Pussy straight. Pizzas and pasta are, after all, very peasanty, very butch and very Mario Batali. Italian desserts, however, are a whole other story. Gelato is always a big gay hit. (Stracciatella simply has to be the name of a drag queen from Puglia.) But those nasty, lurid, sickly sweet, creamy cakes? Too gay for this gay.

By now I'm sure you are getting the general idea: Big fat slabs of wild boar are straight. Duh! And wafer-thin fillets of sole meunière are gay. Ladurée macaroons are at one end of the gay/straight spectrum, and beef Wellington is at the other.

The irony—the raging, screaming paradox—of the gay/straight food divide is that the gayest food—brace yourselves, because this searing insight is really going to send sparks flying out of your lettuce spinner—is produced by *the straightest people*! Did not see that coming, did you, now?

If you are ever presented with an appetizer of mango-braised South Sea scallop, floating on a miniature-cucumber tapenade and garnished with a roulade of fricasseéd sweetbreads and herb-encrusted quenelles of pulverized aardvark ovaries, you can bet your bottom dollar that a big butch heterosexual created it. No self-respecting gay chef would ever give birth to anything so embarrassingly gay.

I encountered this strange paradox when, in 2009, I served as a judge on *Iron Chef*. The two hairy, sweaty, manly competing chefs were Mike Lata and Jose Garces. Sparkling wine was the Secret Ingredient, and I was definitely the gayest person on the set.

As the show began, I braced myself for the butchest gastronomic onslaught of my life. At the very least I expected, based on the look of the chefs, to be eating deep-fried buffalo stuffed with beef cheeks, or Guinness-marinated yak testicles on a bed of wildebeest giblets.

When the food appeared, I was gobsmacked by how gay it was: I have never seen so many tangerine emulsions and champagne gelées in my life. Scratch a butch chef and you'll find a bitch. Everything was a "duo" of this and "lassi" of that. Nothing was served without a mini-artichoke or a micro-dollop of sheep's cheese. Don't get me wrong: I had a total blast. I am merely attempting to shine a spotlight on this foodie conundrum.

Last year I was gourmandizing in the South of France. In the mood for a healthy, balanced meal, I ordered sardines. In my mind I saw a rustic, casual assemblage of grilled, pudgy sardines (straight) nonchalantly hurled onto a mountain of organic greens (gay). *J'adore!*

When the dish arrived, my gay nerves just about snapped: The plate was triangular (gay) and the raw (!) sardines were cut into narrow, perfectly rectangular strips (so gay) and arranged into an abstract basket-weave pattern (Liberace gay). The sauce was a swirl of chartreuse something or other. When le chef appeared to mingle with we diners, all was revealed. He was straight, Sarkozy straight, even Dominique Strauss-Kahn straight. Only a straight chef could have taken a nice, wholesome hetero sardine and transformed it into something so explosively gay. A gay chef would never create anything so poofy and contrived, for fear of being vilified, pelted with stuffed zucchini blossoms and chased out of town.

To further prove my point, let's take a look at the gayest, most extreme trends in foodie culture and find out who is behind them.

Let's start with the most horrifically gay innovation of all time: the foam movement. Goat cheese foam. Truffle foam. Foam foam. It is insupportable! And, you guessed it, foam was invented by some straight dude, a Spaniard named Ferran Adrià.

Why not a gay? No homo chef would ever put himself in the position where somebody was going to say, "Wait. I know you gay guys have lots of sex, but was it absolutely necessary to jizz all over my risotto?" Only a straight dude would have the balls to cum on your food.

The award-winning Señor Adrià has also pioneered the strange art of molecular gastronomy. I cannot really decide if this syringe-wielding, laboratorial genre of cookery is gay or straight. It's sort of sinister and futuristic. One is reminded of Dr. No: maniacal ambitions of world domination (straight), but with a fluffy Persian cat on his lap (très gay).

Almost as hideous: the dry-ice movement. If you go to see Cher or Celine Dion, you expect to see the stage fill up with dry ice. Well, hang on to your poker chips, girls, because you are also going to see it in abundance when you are dining at Tao and Twing and Twang and Twat or any of those louche Las Vegas après-show eateries. The macho Sin City chefs love nothing more than to deliver your pyramid of tuna tartare to your table on a white fluffy cloud of carbon dioxide.

And for dessert? Here we are forced to confront an even more ridiculous seems-totally-gay-but-emanates-from-a-straight-kitchen trend. Ingesting precious gems and metals has become a huge part of the sleazy, macho casino culture. I call it the opulence movement: gold leaf on your ice cream; colloidal silver on your crème brûlée; crushed diamonds in your crêpes. What's next? Miniature bundt cakes topped with molten aluminum?

Why am I ranting on about this stuff?

I am scared of retribution, that's why.

I feel that gay men will at some point be blamed for these egregious foodie follies. And it is simply not our fault. It's the straight dudes! I am just a voice in the wilderness, trying to head off any unpleasant confrontations, and looking out for my poofter brothers.

At the end of the day (when, exactly, is "the end of the day"? I have often wondered) I believe that we should all be eating balanced meals, which involves a healthy combo of both the gay and straight food groups.

To give you a better sense of what I'm talking about, let me walk you through my typical food day.

BREAKFAST

I start the day with *The New York Post* (straight) and a big bowl of fluffy blueberries (gay), over which I drizzle as much All-Bran as will fit in the bowl. Tough, crusty, bowel-scraping fiber is, it is important to note, usually to be found in straight foods such as black beans, oatmeal and volcanic ash.

Beverages? I wash my breakfast down with a piping-hot mug of Kukicha tea. This is a hearty, dark brown twig brew with an infinite array of healthful properties, all of which were unfurled to me by a spotty-faced youth in a health food store in San Francisco many moons ago. I no longer recall what he said, but I have been drinking it for years with no ill effects, and only slightly stained teeth.

LUNCH

Lunch should be blithely gay in summer, and hot and hetero in winter.

In the summer I will concoct a personalized salad at one of the bustling take-out emporiums which are now drizzled throughout the universe. The uber-convenient salad-mixing station is invariably set up so you can easily assort your gay (croutons, snap peas, arugula) and straight (chicken cubes, feta lumps, olives) ingredients.

In the winter I dine on two piping-hot cups of soup, one gay and one straight. For example: one cup of vegetable minestrone (gay) and one cup of hearty chicken noodle (straight). My liquid lunch habit has led to rumors that I am unable to chew because I wear dentures.

DINNER

It's a bisexual thing. I prefer to alternate straight and gay on subsequent nights. Some nights I go gay with a dainty salmon fillet and a dollop of Julienned veggies. (I am not sure who Julienne is, but she is doing a lovely job.) The following night I will rock a superstraight roast chicken with brown rice and thick florets of broccoli. Dessert? I tend to prefer straight desserts, like a hearty, wholesome apple pie. Gay desserts, like the Italian ones mentioned earlier, are too sloppy and sweet and leave me feeling queasy.

Note the wise, thoughtful and figure-enhancing integration of both gay and straight foods in my daily choices. By following this regime I am able to stay slim and trim. Straight men get fat when they go berserk and pig out on straight foods. Gay men don't get fat because they ingest a creative fusion of the two. It's just that simple.

Bon appétit!

JAMIE
OLIVER
IS
a
LESBIAN

I have a great idea for a trendy new food product. It dovetails perfectly with the new wholesome, earnest, sustainable locavore movement. It's organic and hearty and sincere. I'm talking about *lesbian olive oil.*

If you walked into Whole Foods and saw lesbian olive oil lurking on the shelves, would you be able to resist?

Let's dial back.

The year is 1986. I am living in New York City in a charmless high-rise building near Midtown with my pal Robert. Robert and I are what we gays call "sisters," i.e., our relationship is platonic.

I am working at Barneys and Sister Robert works for the fashion designer Rifat Ozbek. In fact, our apartment doubles as the Ozbek showroom. During the day it's full of buyers and press and the occasional future supermodel, including, but not limited to, an astoundingly young and beautiful Naomi Campbell. At night, the buyers and supermodels go home, and we sleep under the rolling racks of clothes.

One wintry Saturday I am snoozing under a canopy of colorful Ozbek creations when the phone rings. It's my sister, my biological sister. She's calling from England to tell me something important. Something very important.

At the age of thirty-five she has become a lesbian.

My first thought is not exactly a profound one.

What will she wear?

Before you lambast me for superficiality, please remember that the seventies and early eighties was the era of "the oatmeal dyke." The lesbian world was still shot through with a bra-burning, feminist anti-fashion. The thought of my petite, sportif and well-dressed sister—she favors Breton sailor tops and spiffy black pants like Jean Seberg in *À bout de souffle*—morphing into a burly, Jazzy-riding, Provincetown bulldagger was worrying, to say the least.

Her lesbian declaration was not exactly what you might call a bolt out of the blue. Clues abounded during our childhood. While I enjoyed playing with dollies, Sheel was always happy to pick up the butch slack and play the tomboy.

As she grew older, the signs became more explicit. At college she dabbled in political activism, attending demos and hearty feminist seminars. While I was turning into Glam Rock Gloria, she was morphing into Hanoi Shelagh.

In the early eighties, though still dating men, she participated in the famous, and very lengthy, Greenham Common action, where hundreds of dungaree-wearing chicks with wedge haircuts formed a human chain around the eponymous army base in an effort to stymie the arrival of the Pershing missiles. Betty Doonan, our drag queen mother—nylons, high heels and full maquillage—would visit occasionally and smoke ciggies with the girls and share not very pacifist anecdotes regarding her Rosie the Riveter years, fighting in the Second World War.

Et voilà! It was, in many ways, a miracle that Shelagh Doonan had waited till her thirties to lezz out.

Somehow I managed to suppress my natural inclination to focus on the fashion ramifications of her new-chosen path and asked a more sensible question.

"Have you told Mum and Dad?"

I was a little concerned about how my parents might be handling what was essentially a fairly massive double gay whammy. Two kids. Two queers. What the fuck did we do wrong kind of a thing. In my mind's eye I saw Betty and Terry barreling out of their retirement bungalow, filling their pockets with rocks and walking into the oily waters of Belfast Lough.

First came moi, a son who was so gay he liked to flit round the backyard, age six, in the style of the Ballet Russe. A son so gay he wore his mum's clothing à la Norman Bates. A son so gay that he became a window dresser. A son so gay that he actually won awards for being a window dresser. A son so gay that, a few years back, he was plonked at the top of *Time Out* magazine's list of "the gayest people in New York City." (The list was not alphabetized. Harvey Fierstein was below me. That's how gay I am.)

And now a lesbian daughter?

My sister sighed. "Dad didn't say much. Mum just said, 'I'm not over the moon.'"

Not over the moon.

I felt a big surge of sympathy. In that moment I understood that being a dyke was somehow more complex than being a poofter. If a boy tells his mother he's gay, she will probably get a bit weepy at first. Ten minutes later he's ratting and styling her hair or rearranging the living-room furniture and they are both shrieking with laughter. But tell your mother you have become a lesbo and everything goes all *Children's Hour*. Everything slides to the floor and disappears down *The Well of Loneliness*. Or at least that's the way it was back then.

In the past, lezzies got a raw deal. Gay women always seemed more mysterious to the general population than we poofters. Let's put this concept into easy-to-understand showbiz terms: Compare Liberace with Nancy Kulp and you will clearly see the difference. Lib was gaudy and flashy and obvious and out there. Nancy was nuanced and enigmatic and strangely unknowable. As preposterous and revolting as male gayness was to society—see *Victim* starring Dirk Bogarde—lezzie activities were deemed to be a thousand times more strange.

While gay men were able to counter prejudice by being chatty and hilarious, carpet munchers always tended to be guarded and remote. Don't get me wrong—I'm not blaming them. With few allies, the lezzies of yore had a rougher time: Straight women felt they were treacherous for abandoning traditional roles. Straight men either ignored them or took a prurient interest in their sex lives and encouraged them to "chow down" with each other for hetero delectation.

Most often a dyke was just regarded with suspicion: it was as if she had become a Wiccan or a Scientologist. Nobody cheered. No encouraging words for you, you lesbian, you. Best-case scenario? Your mom lights up a fag and tells you she's "not over the moon."

So, back then, lesbianical activity enjoyed less acceptance than gay-boy action. Was that the reason why my sister took so long to, as it were, buckle on her sapphic fanny pack?

I asked Sheel about that delay. Why wait so many years for the *grande voilà!* Was it societal antipathy, or was it the anticipation of an *et tu, Brute* response from my parents? First your faggoty-ass, window-dressing brother and now YOU!

She surprised me with her answer.

"I always had certain feelings, but then I went to see that movie, *The Killing of Sister George*, and the depiction of lesbians was so horrible it forced it all back inside and I focused on boys."

This 1968 lezploitation movie, though chock-full of unintentional laughs, is not exactly heartwarming in its depiction of lesbian life. Au contraire! Sister George is a gin-swilling thespian lesbian with a horrifyingly short fuse. She intimidates Childie, her uber-girly girlfriend in all kinds of bizarre ways. (Childie is played by gorgeous Susannah York in a series of chiffon baby-doll nighties, and a tweed-skirted Beryl Reid plays George the gargoyle.) At one point Sister George forces Childie to eat her cigar butt. George also threatens Childie with the ultimate: drinking George's bathwater. My poor sister had seen this movie at a sensitive moment in her late teens, and the histrionics of the principal players had caused her to suppress any lesbo inclinations.

Fast-forward thirty years.

The entire landscape has changed.

Lesbians are the flava du jour.

Since that phone call, I am happy to report that my sister has constructed a fearless lesbian life for herself without becoming either a George or a Childie. In 1998 she met a fabulous social worker/belly dancer/single mom named Anna. On their first date—a blind rendezvous at a rural tea shop—they both wore green polar fleece. *Green polar fleece!*

I know what all you bitchy queens are thinking. You are thinking, "Well, duh! Two dykes? It's really not such a coincidence that they were both wearing green polar fleece."

But here's the crux. Here's the deal. Here's the big shocker-ooni. They were both wearing green polar fleece, *but so was everyone else in the tea shop!*

Everyone on earth is wearing polar fleece because everyone has, at least from a lifestyle point of view, become a raging lesbian.

Pour me a recycled paper cup of that delicious, sustainably harvested, cruelty-free coffee, add a little organic soy milk and I will explain all.

Lesbian is hip. Lesbian is happening. Western culture is now lesbian culture, and vice versa. Our entire society has adopted the crunchy, hearty, alternative values of those dykes of yore. The Green movement—the dominant trend of our age—sprang directly from the loins of those sixties munchers. The core values of the lesbian brand—and yes, it has become a brand—are now shared by all consumers. These values scream wholesome sustainability and fanny packs. (We'll get to them in a moment.)

Now that the lesbian ethos is so dominant in our culture, I have begun to use the word "lesbian" as if it was a commonplace adjective. If people ask me, "How was your weekend in Shelter Island?" I am quite likely to reply, "Very lesbian. We went hiking in the nature preserve and made a brown-rice pilaf. How was yours?" There is no question about it in my mind, lesbian is *comme il faut.* "Lesbian" is the adjective du jour.

Muji: beige lesbian!

Uniqlo: lesbo sportif!

A skinny cargo pant: leggy lesbian!

An artisanal doughnut shop in Brooklyn: yummy lesbian!

"Lesbian," the adjective, is especially resonant when applied to dining out. "Lesbian" calls to mind organic kumquats, eateries with rough-hewn community tables, locally harvested turnips, hand-thrown pickles . . . you get the picture. "Lesbian" speaks to everything which is hearty, wholesome and honest, and what could be more au courant.

This in no way conflicts with the philosophy of glamorous fabulosity which is prescribed and disseminated by we fags. I see it as being separate and complementary.

Faggotism = life-enhancing glamour.

Lesbian = locavore hipster chic.

A hardworking eco-warrior of my acquaintance spends her days making organic olive oil in Spain, using honest, authentic peasanty techniques. Like many gay women she is ultracompetent in the production of her worthy fare. Unfortunately, she is not such a whiz in the marketing department. Give her a mound of organic olives and, before you can say Gertrude Stein, she will grind 'em right up and, before you can say Melissa Etheridge, she will hand you a vat of olive oil, glowing gorgeously in a recycled glass container. But advertising and marketing the stuff? That's not such a lesbian thingy.

How can she market her olive oil? How might she bring it to the attention of the Nigella Lawsons and Jamie Olivers of the world?

The answer is obvious.

She needs to rebrand! She must change the name of her product. She must call it *lesbian organic olive oil.*

I see a nifty new logo, solid, peasanty, with a heritage feel but not too florid. One color. And we can print it—maybe even lino cut! How lesbian is that?—on hand-milled lesbian unbleached locally-pulped paper.

A lesbian tapenade? How salty and hearty would that taste?

Fingers crossed that my pal will see the light and adopt my lesbo-marketing strategy. In the meantime, let's give thanks for the new ubiquity of wholesome, uncontrived lesbian artisanal pickle emporiums. Ditto the ubiquity of bicycles, recycling bins and, most important of all, the return of the fanny pack. I am a big fanny-pack lover. They are convenient, stylish and, if the eighties are back, then so are fanny packs.

Lesbians have stayed loyal to the fanny pack, even during the years when it was the most reviled fashion accessory on earth. They should be applauded for their tenacity and vision. They knew it would come back—you can't keep a good accessory down—and come back it has, with a vengeance. Designers from Reed Krakoff to Alexander Wang have introduced cunning and stylish new iterations of this much-missed accessory.

An important tip: Fanny packs tend, more than regular purses, toward a certain homogeneity. In order to avoid confusion, be sure to be-charm, personalize or embellish yours in some way which clearly differentiates it from those of your pals.

My sister learned this the hard way. Shelagh recently experienced a fanny-pack fiasco. Last spring, she and her friends converged on the house of a friend in South London for an evening of polite discourse and belly dancing. Upon arrival, the gals all dumped their fanny packs on the hostess's bed.

After two or three hours of sisterly conviviality, they returned to their respective homes only to find that their front-door keys no longer seemed to work. It turned out that the dykes had all unwittingly gone home with *the wrong fanny pack*!

How lesbian is that?

GO
TUCK
YOURSELF

Like many gays, I am a deeply spiritual person.

Forced from the confines of traditional religion by my faggotry, I have sallied forth and developed my own philosophy of life. I call it Go Go Fabulosity.

Here are the basic tenets.

I think of life as being like a disco cube. You climb on, you jiggle about a bit and eventually you fall off. It's just not that complicated.

When you are young, you look pretty on your cube. Everyone likes pretty things. They show their appreciation by tucking dollar bills into your panties, metaphorically, of course. As you get older, you start to lose your looks.

Good-bye, looks! Nice knowing ya!

As your looks fade, the dollars turn to coins, and then to tomatoes. If you are lucky, you drop dead and fall off your cube before the tomatoes turn to rocks. C'est la vie! C'est la mort.

The possibility of extending this timeline so that you could stay on your disco cube simply never occurred to me. The notion of dimming the lights slightly, and going right on jiggling like an ingénue, was never part of my philosophy. And the notion of pruning off bits of yourself so that you could look younger and delude everyone into giving you more cube time seems quite sneaky and, dare I say it, ungodly.

The story of Max.

Like every gay man, Max is obsessed with lighting. Tweaking it, adjusting it, bathing in it and, most important, reducing it. When it comes to lighting, he is a latter-day Blanche DuBois.

Like Blanche, Max's main goal in life is to minimize the glare so as to optimize whatever is left of his middle-aged flair. Like Blanche, he has even been known to throw a paper lantern or a peach-colored chiffon scarf over a lightbulb. Anything to flatter the visage!

Dimmer switches are his lifeblood. Max has always relied on the kindness of dimmers. Dimmers are to Max what red corpuscles are to other human beings. Every fixture in his domain is dimmed to a low level of melancholy glamour. Even the toaster has a dimmer. If Max was on life support, he would ask for those big hospital machines that go *ping* to be on a dimmer so that he could control his final fade to black.

Christmas Day, a couple of years back.

I call Max to wish him season's greetings. His cell phone rings forever. I assume he has dimmed the lights to such an extent that his phone is unlocatable. This would not be the first time. Then he answers, sort of.

"Erry issmass!"

His speech is impaired. It almost sounds as if he has duct tape over his mouth. I assume he has been mugged by rough trade (again!). Should I call the police?

"I'm fine. I'm down in Brazil."

"Xmas on the beach?"

"No. I'm in the hospital. I just had a face-lift."

Max's Christmas prezzie to himself was a cut-rate Brazilian makeover: an eye lift, a turkey wattle-ectomy, and a whole butt-load of lipo.

To prove he is alive he has the nurse take a picture of him, waving from the bed. He sends it to me. It is terrifying.

Above the bed hangs a meager garland of tinsel, like those thin feather boas that Janis Joplin used to feature. Max is sporting a fetching floral surgical gown. On his head is a strange white plastic bonnet that recalls the 1960s futuristic creations designed by André Courrèges. The flawless white architecture of the bonnet contrasts dramatically with Max's pulverized visage.

His face looks like a strawberry-blueberry fruit compote.

Merry fucking Christmas!

Max's surgery is a wake-up call to me.

I always thought that face-lifts were just for chicks. Heterosexual women, with their self-critical, masochistic age obsession, seemed more likely, much more likely, to submit to the knife. Straight broads are always looking for ways to tweak what God has given them, especially if it involves pain and parting with large quantities of dough.

In the past, a gal was happy to dollop a mittful of Pond's Cold Cream onto her face and call it a day. Now she stops at nothing in her quest to look like a seventeen-year-old sexy siren: we're talking lipo, skin peels, anal bleaching, fake boobs, vaginal rejuvenation.

But the gays? Did not see that one coming.

Why the blind spot?

Simply put: plastic surgery does not jive with my disco cube Go Go Fabulosity philosophy of life.

It all seems very counterintuitive to me. Why would you want to remain on your disco cube after your sell-by date has expired? How horrid to be stuck up there, all stretched and tortured, hoping nobody will notice your crepey old knees? How horrible to be so embalmed with fillers and Botox, and so sliced and diced, that you have to remain backlit 24/7 or people will just start screaming à la Freddy Krueger whenever they see your face?

I realize I am in the minority. The antiaging movement has gone global. And now Max and the gays have leapt upon the bandwagon. I should have seen it coming. It was inevitable that my homo brothers, with their relentless focus on appearance, would start slicing and dicing.

Clearly, I can't stop y'all from having a little work done but I can offer a few tips and a little cautionary advice: Before you buy that round-trip ticket to Rio, try adjusting your bathroom lighting. Max and Blanche DuBois, though clearly out of their minds, are onto something when it comes to lighting. Before you tweak your visage, tweak your wattage.

That critical moment every morning when you glue on your lashes and pop in your teeth can set the tone for the day.

If the face staring back in the mirror at you looks like Harry Dean Stanton, and you are a woman, then you may wish to pursue a new lighting strategy: Heat it up and dim it down. If the lighting is cold, then warm it up a bit. Your mot du jour is "peach."

Regarding liposuction: Here's a little-known fact, and a word of caution. Whether you are gay or straight, you have only a finite number of fat cells in your body. If, post-lipo, you eat your weight back on, the remaining un-lipoed cells will be obliged to expand. Max, an insatiable gourmand, has been back for more rounds of lipo. As a result, his fat cells, while fewer in number, are getting larger and larger. I imagine that by now they are each about the size of a Tic-Tac. If he keeps going back for more, the dwindling remaining cells will be obliged to further increase in size. They will soon become macaroon size, and then, ere long, bagel size. Eventually, if he keeps up the lipo/gorging cycle, he will have only one remaining fat cell, and it will be the size of the Anish Kapoor bean in Chicago.

Regarding eye lifts: An extraordinary realization hit me while vacationing last summer. There I was, sitting on my deck out in Shelter Island, enjoying a bit of global warming and cruising my new favorite website, menwholooklikeoldlesbians.blogspot.com.

Yes, I was chuckling, but I was also looking for answers. What exactly was making geezers like Jon Voight and Bruce Jenner look so much like old lesbians and, more important, how could I avoid it?

Just as my vexations were reaching a peak, my pal Vickie, a lesbian landscape designer, dropped by to fill me in on the prognosis of a white pine that has been looking a bit peaky of late.

As soon as she had finished opining on my pine, I lobbed the question du jour: "You are a gay woman: Can you please tell me what it is about George Steinbrenner, Tony Curtis and Roy Orbison that makes them look so sapphic and sisterly?"

"It's really quite obvious," she replied, in a why-are-gay-women-so-much-smarter-than-their-male-equivalents kind of a way, "it's the eye lift!"

I realized instantly that—by Georgette!—Vickie was on to

something. A pudgy older guy, or gay, with decreasing testosterone already looks a tad femmy, but the eye lift is the coup de grâce. Anytime an older dude gets a little up-tuck he immediately joins the sisters over in Carpet Village.

And what, you may well ask, is so terrible about looking like an old lesbian. Okay. Nothing. Nada. There's nothing wrong with looking as if you are riding a one-way ticket to the end of the line and the last stop is the Dinah Shore Open. Absolutely nothing. If Al Gore gets an eye lift and turns into Rosie O'Donnell, then so what? I merely wanted you to be aware that this was a distinct possibility. That's all.

Regarding your post-surgery recovery period: Don't be rash with your cash. Max and my other pals who went to Latin America in order to stretch their dollars, and their faces, all came back broke. Those cut-rate face-lifts were a triumph. However, the money my homos saved on surgery they quickly splurged on the godlike "escorts" they encountered on Ipanema beach.

One final chilling thought before you sally forth into the land of rusty scalpels, potential bacterial infections, Lisa Rinna lip redos, unblinking cobralike Cher eyes, Madonna masks, frozen Kidman foreheads, inflated porno hooters, frozen rigor-mortis smiles and Faye Dunaway fillers:

Keep your expectations in the basement.

An eminent plastic surgeon of my acquaintance always warns his clients to minimize their post-surgical hopes and dreams. To illustrate his point, he tells the cautionary tale of a client named Muriel.

Muriel scrimped and saved for her surgery. She even set aside money for a new wardrobe and a post-op recuperation vacation.

When Muriel returned from the Seychelles, she felt reborn. Sun-kissed and rejuvenated, she headed home for Thanksgiving. This would be the *grande voilà!* This would be the first day of the rest of her life!

She timed her arrival so that her entire family would already be seated. As she walked up the driveway, she braced herself for a ticker-tape welcome. The finale of *American Idol* was spooling through her head. Tears. Confetti. A heartfelt toast to the reborn Muriel. Maybe even a prayer!

"Where the fuck have you been?"

"Sit next to Uncle Clyde! And give him some more black-eyed peas."

"Pass the gravy, Muriel . . . and smile for chrissakes!"

"What's the matter? Cat got your tongue?"

The moral of the story: always carry a large "before" picture to family functions.

A
NELLY
on the
TELLY

When Stephen was a young boy, he encountered a pansy on the grounds of his family's country estate and was astounded by its velvety perfection. So astounded was he, in fact, that he fainted right there on the gravel next to the flower bed. Later that same day, Lord Glenconnor, his concerned and rather butch father, asked him what he wanted to be when he grew up. Without too much hesitation, he replied, "Sir, I want to be a great lady," or words to that effect.

The Right Honorable Stephen Tennant lived from 1906 to 1987. Layabout, poseur, eccentric, he was a member of a claque of effete young aristos known as "the Bright Young Things," a group which included Cecil Beaton and the Mitfords and Evelyn Waugh and this one and that one. He wore black rubber trench coats, pounds of makeup, decked his house with shells and fishnets (not the ones you wear, surprisingly) and cut his hair in the latest ladies' style known as *the shingle.*

He was, as you can probably tell, even from this small snippet, a foulard-wearing, bracelet-jangling, palazzo pant–wearing, perfumed poof of mammoth proportions. He was a nelly. Mr. Tennant, God rest his soul, may even have been the nelliest person who ever minced the earth.

Let's, for a moment, play stupid, pretend we all just flew in from Uranus and ask the obvious question: What is a nelly?

A nelly is a specific genre of gay male. Uncompromisingly foppish, unimaginably overdressed and unapologetically superficial, a nelly is a real homo's homo. A nelly makes Oscar Wilde look like Burt Reynolds. A nelly is someone who views life through a gilded, bejeweled lorgnette while standing knee-deep in the red velvet squish of an opera box. A nelly is a languid and limp poofter whose affect is that of a female actress. A nelly idolizes and imitates sassy barroom broads and vampy campy chicks. In other words, a nelly is a fanfuckingtastically charismatic and entertaining human being.

I realize that not everybody shares my enthusiasm for nellies. When straight guys, for example, encounter a nelly, they often become irrationally incensed. Some even experience the impulse to maim and mangle the nelly in question. Nelly aversion is ubiquitous and very central to the issue of homophobia. This gut-level antipathy toward even the minutest smidgen of mannered effeminacy is what causes some to hate gay people and want to strangle them. Something about the sight of a man abandoning guy world and adopting girly stuff has infuriated and discomforted heterosexual dudes throughout history. Could it be that these irate heteros have, at some point or other, experienced, and subsequently suppressed, a whole catalog of girly impulses? I'm not sure. Let's ask Sigmund Freud.

Me: "So, Siggy, darling. What's the deal with nelly persecution?"

Freud: "The motivation is as transparent as a jellyfish. The idea of a nelly gay man succumbing to the lure of a feather boa, and daring to enjoy it, elicits a primitive homicidal reaction in many a straight asshole, because many a straight asshole is wrestling with similar impulses."

Me: "Thanks, Sigmund."

Freud: "You're welcome. My advice to nelly haters is to chillax and enjoy the show."

Me: "Oh, Mr. Freud, I could not have put it better myself. Ciao for now!"

In my opinion, and I am sure Freud would agree with me, everyone on earth needs a nelly in his or her life. Nellies are life enhancing. Nellies bring joy. Even regular gays need nellies. Nellies are nifty, and nellies are inspiringly courageous. To be a real nelly you have to have nerves of steel. It takes guts to be a sissy.

I have been through some fairly nelly periods in my life, and I have the photos to prove it, but I somehow lacked the wherewithal to knock it out of the nelly park on a consistent basis.

I entered a promising nelly phase when I was about ten. My gay best friend Biddie and I used to stage plays in the attic, where my lobotomized granny hung her old-lady knickers to dry when it was raining, which it always was. Every Saturday we would take down Granny's terrifying garments from her attic washing line and pin up a couple of sheets in imitation of a theater curtain. My blind auntie Phyllis also lived in this attic. She and her seeing-eye dog Lassie constituted our audience.

Given the nelly theme here, it behooves me to pause for a moment and elaborate on the fearless nelly majesty that is Biddie, aka James Biddlecombe. Every gay kid needs a gay bestie. Most never get one. I was lucky. I had Biddie.

Blitz Kid, performer, cabaret artiste and pantomime dame—his Widow Twankey is the stuff of legend—Biddie is admired by many for his voice, timing and wit. We have remained pals for over half a century, and I am happy to report that he is still the most amusingly nelly person on earth.

When, in the early seventies, we first fled our crap town and moved to London, Biddie spent long nelly hours sequestered in our squalid one-room apartment bejeweling and bedazzling his drag frocks and nifty glam-rock ensembles. Over time he developed mysterious, twitchy eye problems.

"Go to the doctor, you stupid cunt!" I said in a kind and caring way. (Back then, the Brits all called one another cunts without thinking twice.)

Upon returning home that evening, I found Biddie hunched over a mug of tea in contemplative mode.

"What did Mr. Eye Doctor say?"

"He looked into my eyes with his thingy, then he asked me if I had been working with sequins or beads of any description. I told him that was *all* I had been doing."

"What a clever cunt!"

"He told me I was suffering from a rare condition called sequin blindness and that I needed to lay off for a while."

Biddie had gone sequin blind! In the annals of medical history this must surely be the nelliest ailment on record.

Back to those attic theatricals.

At the dawn of the sixties my mother quickly ditched the big, stiff petticoats of the previous decade. These out-of-date tulle concoctions were versatile: they made great dowager headdresses, dowager bustles and dowager capes for me and Biddie. Small wonder that all of our plays featured the two of us playing—you guessed it—dowagers. Dueling dowagers, death-defying dowagers and/or devilish dowagers. Every play was a Lady Bracknell–off.

As fearless as we were, we never nellied beyond the confines of Granny's knicker-drying attic. I would have loved nothing more than to ride the bus into town in my dowager costume and pick up a few essentials at Woolworths. But I lacked the nelly conviction.

Fast-forward ten years.

Glam rock arrived in the early seventies. David Bowie and Eno and Bryan Ferry gave me carte blanche to get tarted up and nellied up.

The high point of my glam-rock nellydom occurred when we attended the now legendary Bowie concert at the Finsbury Park Rainbow in 1972. Bowie's hair, and Biddie's, was a bright red toilet brush. Mine was a halfhearted amateur peroxide job.

My mother, who spent many waking hours attempting to look as much as possible like Lana Turner, had a high tolerance for nelly affectations. Nevertheless, my new "look" caught her attention and she saw fit to comment upon my appearance as follows:

"Your hair looks like scrambled egg. Maybe, the next time, you should go to Madge down the road, and have it done professionally instead of hanging round the house with foil on your head looking like Topsy."

She was right. I was tragic.

After glam rock came a retro period—a very Stephen Tennant period, in fact—when my pals and I all smoked lurid-colored cocktail cigarettes out of long Holly Golightly cigarette holders, listened to Gertie Lawrence, watched old Busby Berkeley movies, and plastered down our hair with Biba Brilliantine in an effort to make it look painted on. When we walked into Biba on Kensington High Street to buy the pots of Brilliantine—when I say "buy" I do of course mean "steal"—we tried as hard as possible to look like those languid, elegant art deco sculptures of attenuated men and women being dragged down the street by two anorexic Afghan hounds. Somehow I never quite pulled it off. I just wasn't nelly enough.

In the early eighties, the New Romantics arrived and nelly went postal. Never has there been such a global embrace of foppery and frippery: Culture Club, Spandau Ballet, Steve Strange, and Adam Ant arrived and everyone, straight or gay, began dressing like a Regency poof, or a great lady, or an Otto Dix painting, or all of the above. The entire universe went nelly. The maquillaged magnificence of Boy George brought nelly into the hearts and homes of the un-nelly masses and opened their eyes to the beauty of idiosyncrasy and eccentricity.

I was a cautious participant in this trend. At the time I was living above a garage in downtown Los Angeles, part of the vanguard of the Downtown Renaissance. The neighborhood was thick with intimidating cholo gang boys. My interactions with these lads were always cordial. However, I was disinclined to test their limits by mincing through the 'hood in my Vivienne Westwood pirate outfit. As a result, I used to drive to West Hollywood and get changed in the Ralphs supermarket parking lot on Sunset Boulevard before heading to Club Lingerie. I was clearly no Boy George. I was a fraud. A faux nelly.

To be a real hard-core nelly requires a fearlessness that I simply do not possess. I am, however, very drawn to nellies. They possess a car-crash recklessness which I find truly inspiring.

I am fortunate to have met some extraordinary nellies during my life, including but not limited to Erté, Bunny Roger, Tony Duquette, George Melly, Boy Marilyn and Pete Burns.

I once had a noteworthy nelly encounter with the late great Quentin Crisp.

"When War was declared, I went out and bought two pounds of henna." So wrote the flame-haired Mr. Crisp in his 1968 autobiography, *The Naked Civil Servant*. I read it avidly upon publication and swore that, one happy hennaed day, I would contrive to meet its brilliant author.

By the early eighties Quentin Crisp had moved to New York City and was living Downtown. Though not in reduced circumstances, thanks to the success of his books, he was not exactly living high on the hog. Somehow, Mr. Crisp managed to let it be known that he was socially available. Quentin, it was generally understood, was happy to eat dinner with anybody. All you had to do was pay.

A friend and I invited him to the Odeon. He arrived exactly on time, looking very like my mother. He and Betty Doonan had the exact same upswept 1940s hairdo. Like Betty he had abandoned the hair coloring of his youth—henna for him and peroxide for her—and was now a distinguished Brillo Pad gray.

There were some important differences.

While Betty Doonan was scrupulously clean, Quentin was—how shall I say this politely—a little dusty. His long fingernails were, if not black, then definitely chocolate brown. His frothy "white" foulard had definitely seen brighter days. And his pancake maquillage, to which was adhered all manner of New York City grit, was the color of concrete.

This lack of persnicketiness should not have come as a big surprise. Mr. Crisp's laissez-faire regarding ablutions and housework were legendary. In his autobio, Quentin, the lifelong bohemian, inveighs against conventional notions of cleanliness: "There was no need to do any housework at all. After the first four years the dirt doesn't get any worse."

We ordered dinner and Quentin settled in to amuse us. Like Scheherazade, he was programmed to entertain with witty anecdotes and tales of his new life in New York City. Top of mind was the fact that he was, at the time of our meeting, receiving the unwanted attentions of a female stalker.

This brassy lady was following him whenever he left his apartment building. Suspecting that, in my broad range of acquaintances, I might know the person in question, I asked for details of her appearance.

"She wears fishnet stockings of such a large mesh," he said, representing a four-inch-wide diamond shape in the air with his two thumbs and two forefingers, "that any fish, of any species and of any size, could pass comfortably through them and find freedom on the other side."

His manner when describing this acolyte was both sinister and haunting. To this very day, lo over thirty years later, I still find myself staring at any old Downtown broad in fishnets, wondering if she was "the one."

By the time he popped his clogs, Mr. Crisp had achieved a not inconsiderable level of transatlantic notoriety. His memorial filled the Great Hall at Cooper Union. This was unusual for the nellies of Quentin's generation. The pre-Internet nellies of yore had no real platform. Now, thanks to YouTube and reality television, nellies are finally moving front and center. From Adam Lambert to *RuPaul's Drag Race* to Mr. Leave Britney Alone! to all the Gaga and Beyoncé imitators, nellies can cavort their way directly into our living rooms.

The Lord Queen Nelly of this new generation of telly-nellies is . . . klieg lights! . . . Mr. Bobby Trendy.

For many happy souls—among whom I enthusiastically numbered myself—Mr. Trendy was a Sunday-night post-*Sopranos* illicit treat and quite possibly the nelliest person to arrive in the living rooms of wholesome Americans.

Hired by the mysteriously spacey and now deceased Anna Nicole Smith to glamorize her California home with his signature gushy satins and feather-trimmed leopard pillows, Bobby Trendy the decorator added a much-needed piquancy to the otherwise turgid vacuum of the former GUESS model's water-treading reality TV show. (She was awaiting the receipt of a multimillion-dollar final settlement after a long and bitter suit with the relatives of her deceased husband, J. Howard Marshall of Houston, Texas.)

An early episode showed Ms. Smith lugging her husband's ashes home and waddling from room to room as she earnestly procrastinated about their placement. It was like watching a fabulous Joe Orton nelly farce. The cocktail-shaker-sized urn containing half the man she married (when he was eighty-nine and she was twenty-six) ended up, much to the horror of the Marshall family, perched on top of the TV next to a particularly mundane arrangement of flowers. At the request of the Marshall family, the urn, along with the labels on Ms. Smith's endless snacks and beverages, was discreetly pixilated whenever it made subsequent appearances.

Bobby Trendy's on-screen appearances were nuclear nelly and the very opposite of pixilated. The pert Mr. Trendy is the queen of the taciturn sound bite. Part *Gong Show*, part Gong Li, he dispensed his nutty utterances with a blank affect that was wildly at odds with their often bitchy content.

I decided I had to meet him.

During the run of the show, I made the pilgrimage to his home-furnishings store in West Hollywood. On a scorchingly hot Saturday, I found Mr. Trendy surrounded by swagged furniture, glossy black cock feathers, burgundy velvets, shocking-pink satins and acolytes of various genders.

"I used to be Vietnamese. But now I am a white woman," said Mr. Trendy, adjusting his diamond-encrusted lady's Chanel watch. "A very rich, very beautiful white woman." I soon discover that Bobby, though decidedly withholding about mundane information, is only too willing to deadpan me with outrageously nelly responses. After several minutes of questioning, all I can really gather about his background is that he was raised in Valencia, in Southern California, and did time as a five-dollar-per-hour cashier at Kmart and as a fashion designer. Like most rich white women, he admitted to being twenty-four years old.

I asked about the décor of his childhood bedroom, hoping this might indirectly shed some light on his past. "It was very normal," the haughty, long-necked Mr. Trendy replied unconvincingly. "Everything in my room was very, very pink because I was very, very feminine."

I asked Mr. Trendy if he was conscious of his enigmatic, sphinxlike demeanor. "What the hell is sphinxlike?" hissed Mr. Trendy in a breathy, sibilant voice. "I don't have emotion. I'm a godlike statue-essssssssssss."

He creepily stroked one of the gold-painted Egyptian plaster cats adorning his chaotic lair, prompting me to ask him about his spiritual life. "Cha-ching! Cha-ching!" he ejaculated quietly, doing what I soon realized was his signature imitation of a cash register.

"I like money and things I can see and touch. I'm not spiritual. I'll leave that to Madonna and her kabbalah. Cha-ching!" On the last "Cha-ching!" Mr. Trendy dove in under a swagged brocade ottoman and pulled out a Burberry box with a pair of the season's must-have rain boots printed in signature Burberry plaid. "See, I'm a clothing whore," he announced. "And I just bought next season's Chanel après-ski boots too."

Mr. Trendy's regal demeanor—Suzie Wong meets Caligula—served him well when dealing with the slobs on *The Anna Nicole Show*. I complimented him on his ability to confront his on-screen, mood-swing-prone employers, and asked him to give me some client-management tips which I might pass along to the interior-decorating professionals among my pals.

"Lip gloss by Lancôme," Mr. Trendy said, without missing a beat. "I smother my lips in lip gloss until I look like a clown. Then everybody listens to everything which comes out of my mouth."

I attempted to shift the conversation in the direction of aesthetics. Many of the scrolled, oversize boudoir pieces displayed in the salon are covered in leopard print (he called it "leper print"). I asked if he was an admirer of the late Diana Vreeland, the iconic fashion editor whose office was all leopard, all the time.

"Diavree . . . ? What's that?" Mr. Trendy said. "A new type of strep throat?"

What book is he currently reading? "I haven't read a book since Dr. Seuss," he said proudly. "I don't read—I teach lessons. I taught Carmen Electra how to use her credit card. Cha-ching! Cha-ching!"

Carmen Electra, Usher Raymond, Janet Jackson and Fernando Vargas have all cha-chinged *chez* Bobby, and judging by the endless phone calls and the frantic visitations by upholsterers and feather wholesalers, business was booming. "Yes, I sell very, very expensive pillows," purred Bobby into his cell phone (which he answered about twenty times during our chat). "They are stuffed with real kookoo feathers, and they are one thousand dollars. Cha-ching!" Click!

The exotic claustrophobia of Maison Trendy and the deranged evasiveness of the proprietor were pushing me toward a reckless line of questioning. I asked Bobby if he'd ever thought about pursuing a minimalist style.

"I don't think about it at all. I'd rather put twenty couches in a room instead of one. Cha-ching! Cha-ching! Cha-ching!"

"Are you descended from the Cha-ching Dynasty?" I joked

feebly, trying to bring a smile to that implacable face. Mr. Trendy ignored me completely and leapt over a chartreuse-colored panne velvet couch to greet a client, a young blond lady with heavy lipliner. "Here's one of my socialites!" While he took yet another cell-phone call, I asked the newly arrived "socialite"—a loan officer from Seal Beach—how she came to pick Bobby Trendy. "I saw him on TV. Isn't he fabulous?" she said.

Mr. Trendy told me that this gal is typical of the adoring "socialites" who now constitute his client/fan base.

"They love me," he said, "because I have a tight face and a tight ass and I'm a rich white woman."

I asked if his furniture brings sensual empowerment to his female clients: Is he a feminist decorator at heart? "I feel like a woman and I live like a woman—is that what you mean?" he replied.

The more I bombarded him with questions, the more insanely goalpost-moving his replies became.

Does he see a therapist?

"I tell other people what is wrong with them—I teach lessons every day."

Mr. Trendy bragged of dining nightly on filet mignon; does he fear mad cow disease? "I repel all diseases."

Now drunk with the hilarity of Monsieur Trendy's nelly Dada responses, I revved up the gravitas: Should America invade Iraq?

"Why? Aren't we getting along?"

Bioterrorism?

"Is that some new type of shampoo which I should know about?"

Maybe this is, after all, the real Bobby—a wickedly nelly version of the Peter Sellers character in *Being There*, a defiant little spitfire who is playing the celebrity game on his own naughty little terms. God knows he's a hell of a lot more fun to interview than the average suppressed straight celebrity: he reveals and appalls in a way that no celeb would dare, and yet, ultimately, he gives away far less.

When I accompanied a heavily made-up and fur-clad Mr. Trendy out onto the La Cienega sidewalk for his photo shoot, adulation poured forth from the northbound traffic. There were no hurled tomatoes or anti-nelly shouts of "Die, faggot!" Only an unmitigated pro-Bobby chorus. Every car that passed his West Hollywood store contained at least one person excitedly mouthing his name, pointing and craning his or her neck toward the art-nouveau letters on the awning. At one point, a huge city bus packed with homeward-bound blue-collar types made an unscheduled stop in front of Bobby's store. The amply bosomed African American driver flung open her doors, screeched, "Hey, Bobby? Quit hot-gluin' them pillows!" and then roared off while her jubilant cargo cheered and waved.

"I like to get fucked everyday, and I don't care who does it," Bobby told me, while being shot. "They can be in a wheelchair or a stroller—I don't care. I don't even bother to look over my shoulder and see who is doing it. I wouldn't want to strain my neck."

As the photo shoot progressed, Mr. Trendy got looser: wielding a flashlight, he even implored the cameraman to "photograph my beautiful butt-hole."

In an attempt to neutralize Mr. Trendy's rising libido, I asked him how much he'd have to be paid to have sex with Anna Nicole. "I may be a white woman, but I'm not a lesbian," he said. "However, money talks . . . so how about one hundred billion dollars? Cha-ching!"

My encounter with Bobby left me more convinced than ever of nelly power and the value of being nelly-adjacent whenever possible. As with Lady Gaga or Daphne Guinness or Isabella Blow, reckless eccentricity and nelly glamour make the world a more challenging, unconventional and interesting place. You need a nelly in your life because all that nelly fearlessness is contagious and empowering.

Keep in mind that the psychic stresses of being a nelly are huge. When a nelly crosses your path, you should treat him with sacred-cow respect and reverence. Always offer a foot rub or a bonbon. Remember, you are in the presence of a mystic, of sorts. And never let a nelly, no matter how sylphlike, slip through your fingers.

OPERATION
GOLDILOCKS

My friend Clarisse works in a mental institution, a hard-core public loony bin. Every day she deals with psychotic people. This is a thankless task. Some patients try to assault her. Some think they are dogs and bark at her. Some even go so far as to ridicule Clarisse's hair, makeup and fashion choices. Here is a direct quote from one of her bitchiest patients: "When I get out of this dump, Dr. Clarisse, I am going to buy myself some moderately priced boots, just like yours."

This is not her first challenging job. Clarisse and her moderately priced boots have always had a knack for finding nerve-racking occupations. Before she became a psychologist, she worked for ten years as an event coordinator on one of those rowdy party boats which circle Manhattan. During the summer months I would rarely see Clarisse. She was married to that boat. Her time was not her own. Every night was a different fiesta of some description or other. One night she would host a high school prom, the next night it would be a bar mitzvah, and then a Hungarian polka situation.

One hot Saturday back in the mid-nineties, I met an exhausted Clarisse for lunch. It was late August and the season had taken its toll on her. There had been a knife fight at her annual Jamaican Rastafari party the night before. The police had been called.

"What about tonight?"

"Tonight will be easy. It's the Bears. I love them. They are great tippers. The only drag is the cleanup afterward. There's so much cum all over the floor that the cleaning people often refuse to deal. I usually end up mopping the jizz myself. But at least there are no knife fights. Pass the Grey Poupon, please . . ."

Bears? Cum all over the floor? Great tippers?

I had no idea what she was talking about. To make things still weirder, Clarisse was making all these appalling statements as if they weren't appalling.

I will be cleaning up Bear cum tonight.

What kind of cum will you be cleaning up?

Over a dessert of sloppy crème brûlée, Clarisse explained everything. The Bears were a new gay subculture. Hairy and prone to wearing dungarees with nothing on underneath, they reminded her of John Goodman, but with beards and shorter hair. And they were fat. Some of them were very, very fat. The normal head count for Clarisse's boat was 150. For the Bear parties, she reduced it to ninety-five "because the Bears are so fucking obese."

This was my first encounter with Bear culture. This was my where-were-you-when moment for the Bear phenomenon. It sticks in my mind because of the cum.

Since that long-ago lunch, the Bear movement has proven to be anything but a passing fad. Bears have become a global phenomenon. There are Bear clubs and bars and Bear events in every country around the world, from Bearcalona in Spain to Mountain Bear Madness in Virginia. There are Bear movie and book festivals, online Bear sitcoms. Academics now write pretentious journals and PhD theses about Bear culture. There's even a band of Bear musicians called Bearapalooza.

A 2007 study, quoted in the Harvard *Gay and Lesbian Review*, claims there are now 1.4 million Bear-identified men in the United States. If so, this is the biggest gay movement in history. This is bigger than Judy Garland, Act-Up, fisting, or wearing Izod shirts in the seventies. This is bigger than rainbow suspenders and butt plugs.

And yet Bear culture is still no more visible to the general population than it was to me back in the nineties. Ask the average person today if he/she is aware of these furry funsters and you will find yourself forced into a long and gruesome explanation, often involving cum, at the end of which your listeners will still be blinking with incomprehension. It's a bearnigma.

As you have probably already gathered, stuffing the word "bear" into every other word in the dictionary is one of the principal bearcupations.

For the purposes of this book, I decide to stage a Bear hunt. Gay men do get fat and they do it willingly, blissfully and deliriously and I want to find out why. I want to wrap my head around this mysterious phenomenon and find out what makes Bears tick, and what makes them eat.

Why, in a world where thinness and ripped physiques are so universally exalted, have these husky hedonists opted to go in the other direction? Was this just a flimsy pretext for seed spilling and piggish gourmandizing? Or was there more to it?

As I embark on this anthropological foray, I must confess to a certain level of trepidation. The idea of surrounding myself with jizzing overweight bacchanalian Bears causes me concern. Whenever I Google anything Bear-related, I am invariably funneled into a vortex of raunchy bearotica: these images of mountainous hairy dudes shagging each other's brains out, and cuming all over somebody's nice new carpet, do nothing to decrease my anxiety.

Most Bears are at least twice my size. I have visions of being accidentally crushed to death, or mistaken for a light snack. The Bears are a whole lotta gay, and a whole lotta straight. Somehow, they manage to embody both the scary libidinal excesses of the gays with the even scarier belligerent, beer-guzzlin', wife-beatin', redneck-trucker aesthetic of the worst kind of straight men. Simply put: I am intimidated.

Stick me in a room with Valentino, Karl Lagerfeld and Tom Ford and I am quite jolly and content. Throw me in a bar with a bunch of giant pig-fuckers in flannel shirts and I start to get a moist crack.

As I begin my Bear hunt, I see myself as a gay Timothy Treadwell, the batty but good-natured Long Islander whose final days frolicking among the Alaskan grizzlies are recorded in the Werner Herzog documentary *Grizzly Man*.

Mr. Treadwell spent thirteen summers studying, and recklessly over-anthropomorphizing these beasts, only to be ingested by one right before hibernation season in early October 2003. His backpack and several body parts were later recovered from the digestive tract of the rogue bear.

I am determined to learn from Tim's mistakes. The last thing

I want to do is end up, Goyard man-bag and all, in the gizzard of a Bear.

The logical place to start my research is by attending a Bear event. There is a truly dizzying array of options, in every country around the world at every minute of every day. And, unlike their ursine namesakes, human Bears do not hibernate. You can literally spend your entire life going from Bear gathering to Bear gathering.

As I peruse these online photo galleries of previous events, my anxieties increase. There they are, fat, hairy and smashed, knocking back beer, rubbing bellies. I try to imagine myself skipping through the crowd, notebook in hand, asking probing questions, and I cannot. There is no chance in hell they are ever going to break off from their activities to chat with *petit* moi.

If I am going to penetrate this subculture, I need a different strategy.

I decide to conduct one-on-one interviews. If I meet with these burly gays individually, I will be much more likely to gain some meaningful insight into this mysterious world. Three Bear encounters should do it.

Operation Goldilocks begins.

THE GINGHAM BEAR

I am shocked. Prior to meeting, I had visions of watching him scarf down two pizzas. He surprises me by ordering a ladylike duck salad. I am meeting my first Bear and already I am stereotyping. I make a mental note to be more objective going forward.

"My dad's nickname was The Bear," says Patrick of New York City. Before I can leap in and accuse him of having a repressed erotic fixation on his own father, he adds, "But I don't have a daddy fixation. My boyfriend is younger than me."

Pictures of Patrick and his boyfriend appear on countless Bear social sites: "In the Bear community we fashion ourselves as socialites. We joke that we're celebribears."

This is by no means Patrick's first moment in the spotlight.

"At college I was a performance artist. Chris Burden was my big inspiration. I would put out fires with my chest."

Patrick, who is five feet ten and weighs 220 pounds, also created a public art installation which required him to hang upside down by his feet from a noose while a video of gay-inversion therapy played on an adjacent screen.

Despite the edgy backstory, I find Patrick to be fresh faced and wholesome, with an endearingly old-fashioned air of dignity and rectitude. It's hard to imagine him wanking all over your Axminster just for kicks.

Patrick is thirty-four but entered Bear world when he was twenty-one. "I always wanted to have a beard," he says. "I liked hairy and not necessarily thin men."

He first found them at The Eagle in Tampa, Florida: "The bar was full of muscle Cubs and muscle Bears."

Bear culture, as I was about to learn, has a complex tribal structure.

Bears: hairy and burly guys.

Cubs: possibly younger, less hairy and/or smaller Bears.

Wolves: lean, hairy older men, sometimes Bear chasers.

Otters: younger versions of Wolves.

Muscle Bears: hairy, buff and burly.

Muscle Cubs: the same but younger and/or smaller.

Panda Bears: Asian Bears.

Polar Bears: Think Santa.

As I nibble on a fava bean, I start to wonder where, in this Disney-esque orgy of furry equivalence, I myself might fall. An undersized, nonthreatening gay dude with gray hair? Surely I must be a Chinchilla.

I ask Patrick how he would classify himself.

"Oh. I'm a Gingham Bear. No question about it. I have a nine-foot closet filled with gingham button-downs, pink, blue, yellow . . ."

Leave it to the gays to fetishize the unfetishizable! Patrick elaborates on the majesty and multiple resonances of gingham.

"It's preppy, but it's also Western and folksy. When I see gingham, I think 'picnic!'"

The perky gingham shirts favored by Patrick and his pals are a codified style fuck-you to the rougher, camo cargo pant–wearing, archetypal Bears. At the time of our interview, he has just returned from Bear Week, the annual Provincetown gathering. Patrick and his gingham claque caused a frisson of indignation when they showed up at the So-wrong Party (Bears are encouraged to wear sarongs) in their crisply ironed ginghams.

"This was our silent protest."

These clubby factions and frictions are a reminder that the Bear movement has been around for more than twenty years. Splinter groups are inevitable.

Patrick enjoys his gingham separatism, but is nonetheless an enthusiastic Bear with a passion for attending Bear clubs and Bear events.

"Back in college, I never went to spring break. Bear Week is my spring break."

His fearless bearplorations and bearcations have brought him to some improbable locations. Patrick has wandered down dark alleys on the outskirts of Taipei to find Bear bars. He has taken late-night strolls around the gardens of Lima in search of co-fetishists. One of his favorite hangouts is a Bear club in the Marais neighborhood of Paris. It's called Le Bear's Den.

Patrick and I are now on dessert. The waiter brings us a pile of polenta cookies. I encourage him to wrap a few in a napkin and save them for later. An image flits through my mind of Patrick waking up during hibernation enjoying a nibble.

It's time to ask the elephant-in-the-room question.

Why?

Patrick is reluctant to ascribe a complex raison d'être to his Bear lifestyle.

"For me it's just about camaraderie. There are still a few bitchy queens, but in general the Bear world is more accepting than mainstream gay culture."

I ask Patrick if there is a bearspeak word to identify a bitchy queen. He says no. I suggest that a bitchy queen should be called a Civet. I seriously start to wonder if I might not be more of a Civet than a Chinchilla. We chuckle. Patrick has a sense of fun about his community. I feel I can address the intrinsic hilarity of it all without offending him.

"What do you call a sexy but morbidly obese Bear?"

"A Hot Ton," replies Patrick in a hot second. "And there's no shortage of them. Keep in mind that the Bear movement overlaps with the feeder/gainer community."

Feeder/gainer?

"Guys who get off helping others pork up."

In my head I suddenly hear the voice of my dad. He was a Second World War vet who had a rough life. Whenever he encountered any contemporary kinkiness, he would always say the same thing: "You need lots of free time in order to become a real pervert. In my day we were always too busy earning a living. I'm jealous."

I ask Patrick about the Bear reputation for drug-fueled shagging.

"Sure, some guys hook up eight times a day and snort crystal meth. My Bear friends are more about pot and—hello!—the munchies. But there are always hos in every group. Once I was leaving a party and I ducked into the coatroom to get my jacket. There were twenty naked Bears having sex. My coat was under one big guy who was getting a blow job. I pulled it out from under him and he just kept going."

I ask Patrick about the future.

"Bears often used to be middle-aged, because only middle-aged people get fat in mainstream culture. Now America is getting fatter. And the Internet has given structure to the movement. Believe me, it is only getting bigger."

Given the burgeoning scope of the movement, how would Patrick explain its invisibility to straights?

"The look is totally average. It incorporates the most common attributes of blue-collar masculinity. Masculinity is not rare. It's conventional. Go to Home Depot and everyone looks like a Bear."

THE FASHION BEARS

They describe their look as "nerdy science teacher," but it's really much more intense, especially given the fact that there are two of them: Tweedle Bear and Tweedle Bear. Bluto times two.

They are the Bear equivalent of the twins in Kubrick's *The Shining*. With their check shirts, suspenders, work boots, thick beards and bulging Bear bellies, these six-foot-tall dudes resemble homicidal Midwestern farmers, the kinds of blokes who tear their livelihood out of the dirt with their Bear/bare hands. And yet, the only thing these two dudes ever tear with their bare hands is silk jersey, and even that is a bit unlikely. They would much rather use a nice, clean pair of pinking shears.

They are Fashion Bears. They make frocks. In fact, they make very beautiful frocks. Their names are Jeffrey Costello and Robert Tagliapietra.

Fashion Bears? This represents something of a paradox. Bear culture frequently positions itself as an alternative to the sleek superficiality and shallow, tacky, vain, narcissistic consumerism of mainstream gay culture, i.e., people like me. Bears laud everything woodsy, outdoorsy, earthy, manly. It is the antithesis of the foofy world of fashion, i.e., my world.

Bear culture may not be hospitable toward fashion, but La Mode has certainly taken to Costello Tagliapietra.

The reason for this is quite simple: the fashion world has always adored an extreme look. Jeffrey and Robert, and the surrealism of their matching, cartoony masculinity, are nothing if not visually compelling. As a result, they have been taken to the bosom. Anna Wintour loves them.

Jeffrey Costello and Robert Tagliapietra reside on the top floor of a ramshackle apartment house in Brooklyn, far from *Vogue* HQ. Their live/work apartment is jammed with the accoutrements of dressmaking: paper patterns festoon the walls. There are bolts of sample fabric, and frocks. Fluid frocks. Filmy frocks.

I dive into a rack and start checking out the luscious silks and exquisite prints of the spring 2012 collection.

"Our look is very Michelle Pfeiffer in *Scarface*," says Robert, the more obviously Italian of the two.

"And of course Faye Dunaway in *Chinatown*, and Shelley Duvall in *Three Women*," says Jeffrey, adding, "We like feminine fragility and yet we look like Zach Galifianakis. Go figure."

Robert and Jeffrey chuckle in unison, their large bellies bouncing comfortably up and down in unison.

Zach Galifianakis is one of several fat, hairy, straight celebrities who have unwittingly become Bear pinups. Others include Mario Batali, Zac Efron, G.I. Joe and the dude on the Brawny paper towel ads.

I ask the lads about their first encounter.

Jeffrey: "We met back in 1994 at The Sound Factory. That was when gay culture was gym culture."

Robert: "Back then we were pseudo-twinks and so much thinner than we are now. Our Bear pals look at pictures of us back then and say, 'OMG, you were actually thin.' But, guess what, back then, in our trendy group, we were considered fat. I was the sweaty, fat Italian."

Jeffrey: "When we started our fashion line, publicists told us we had to lose weight."

Robert: "We were right to ignore them. It was only when we let ourselves be ourselves that stuff started happening."

Jeffrey: "We sent a ten-piece look book to *Vogue*."

Robert: "Anna liked our honesty and integrity. This is who we are. And, most important, she liked our dresses."

I ask the guys how such hairy, burly dudes can produce such spectacularly feminine garments.

"With our Bear paws," says Robert.

Time to get heavy. I ask the boys to reflect on the meaning of Bear culture. Is it just a flimsy pretext for a lot of finger-lickin' fun?

Jeffrey: "You have your sexaholics and your monogamous peeps, just like any other group."

Their favorite event is called Spooky Bear, the Provincetown Halloween shindig. Robert and Jeffrey always concoct an ensemble look.

Robert: "We made matching pointy red felt hats and went as giant garden gnomes."

Jeffrey: "A friend of ours painted his face green and went as the Bear Witch Project."

Robert and Jeffrey have an aura of happy self-acceptance and contentment. There is none of the self-loathing and rage which has characterized previous generations of *Boys in the Band* gays.

Jeffrey: "Gym queens of the eighties and nineties were traumatized into body fascism by AIDS. They were freaked out and justifiably so."

Robert: "Women battle it out with themselves over physical stuff every day. Gay men used to do that. The Bear movement gets rid of that vanity and masochism."

What about their health? When I look at those images of Bear events, all I can think is "sponsored by Lipitor."

Sleep apnea? Heart disease?

Robert: "We both have low cholesterol and low blood pressure. Our doctor is annoyed that he cannot drum up any reasons why we should lose weight."

As I schlep down the stairs from their cozy pad I feel more than a tinge of envy. I am part of the traumatized, gym-addicted generation of poofters Jeffrey was referring to, *and* I have high cholesterol.

THE BLASÉ BEAR

....

Twelve years ago Seymour happened upon Lazy Bear, the annual Bear fest in Guerneville, near the Russian River, and his life was changed forever. This tall, redheaded driving instructor from the Midwest had a bearpiphany.

"It was paradise. I could not believe that there were all these guys running around half-naked and woofing at each other, and at me, and they were all my type. Hot, hairy and horny."

"Woof!" is the standard Bear greeting and, from what I can gather, suggests that the woofer would like to cuddle the woofee as soon as possible.

Woofing aside, it was the cheeky playfulness of the event which made the biggest impression on Seymour, and in particular the shocking and boisterous ritual known as Bear Soup.

"At one point on the last day, all the Bears crashed into the swimming pool and faced in the same direction, and then they began to pogo up and down in unison."

All this seismic activity created a roiling, boiling choppiness.

On this particular occasion, according to Seymour, the Bears got quite carried away. They bobbed up and down with such enthusiasm that they displaced half the water from the pool. A virtual tidal wave of Bear Soup flooded the lobby of the resort.

Seymour loved it. It was beartopia.

"In New York or Chicago I always felt invisible. At Lazy Bear, I was suddenly Bear nip. I was chased from one end of the resort to the other, mostly by Polar Bears! Woof!"

Bear culture is commendably inclusive. Everyone, no matter how old or fat, has a shot. Even super-femmy Bears.

"Sometimes you see a hot, hairy guy, you both start talking and five thousand Chanel handbags come flying out of his mouth," says Seymour, striking some uncharacteristically nelly attitudes, adding, "These guys are known as Lady Bears."

New Bear categories pop up all the time. This year, Seymour met a whole group of guys who called themselves Doughnut Bears. An even bigger group—they rode the streets of P-town on motorized Jazzies—were dubbed the Planets "because they were so fucking huge and they were orbiting about."

While Seymour has an infinite tolerance for fat, the same is not true for hair or, rather, hairlessness. Like the vast majority of Bears, he is in hot pursuit of the hirsute.

"I met a handsome Native American Indian at P-town Bear Week. He just kept apologizing because he had no body hair. It became annoying. He had a Chihuahua. Maybe he should have glued it to his chest."

Though overwhelmingly positive about Bear culture, Seymour is also capable of objective criticism.

"The Bear community has changed since the early, naive days. Now it can be just as bitchy as the movement it was reacting against. Unless you have the specific look—cargo pants, Bear tee—you are not considered hot by some Bears."

Seymour also objects to the commercialization of the original Bear concept.

"I get annoyed by those stupid T-shirts that say, 'Dip me in honey' and 'You had me at woof.' The same thing happened to the counterculture. One minute it was real, the next minute boring housewives in the Midwest were dressed up as hippies for Halloween."

Seymour's biggest criticism is directed toward a certain maturity level.

"Most of the Bears I meet now are very boyish, and not in a good way. I don't think they ever read a newspaper. They play video games and collect Simpsons dolls and their idea of a great night out is to head to the opening of some 3-D superhero movie. Like the two fat, retarded guys on the Sarah Silverman show."

Seymour's nostalgia for the early years is waxing rather than waning.

"When Bear Week started, it was way more folksy. There were ice-cream socials and clambakes. Now it's all about druggy circuit parties that cost fifty bucks."

Though Seymour remains Bear identified, he no longer attends the bigger events. He stopped after a particularly traumatic occurrence last Halloween. He showed up at a costume party in his native Chicago wearing an elaborate unicorn costume, complete with a three-foot-long rainbow-painted glitter horn. He was the only Bear who had bothered to dress up.

On this rather poignant note I leave Seymour. He has a date with a Polar Bear, and I don't want to come between this interspecies coupling.

As I scurry through the streets, some young thug calls me a faggot. It happens every so often. On this occasion I can't help wishing I was a big fat Bear, a Hot Ton, or even a Planet. I would climb off my Jazzie and squash the shit out of him.

This kind of assault, I reflect, would never happen to a Bear. By adopting that brutish, hetero, aggressively un-gay disguise, they have created a safe space where they can live happily and cum all over the carpet whenever they feel like it.

You go, girls!

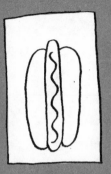

GAY
MEN
DO EAT
CRUMBLE

"You fat fucking pig! I cannot believe you ate all my rhubarb crumble."

While I was regaling our two dining companions with what I felt sure was an utterly hilarious anecdote, my Jonny had snuck in and eaten the rest of my dessert, right under my nose. The audacity! He took advantage of a particularly bubbly and vivacious moment in my storytelling—I cannot exactly remember the thrust of the narrative but I do remember that, at this particular juncture, my arms are waving in the air—and zipped in for the kill using his fork. It was a total stealth attack. I responded to this assault in what seemed to me to be a perfectly normal way: I called him a fat fucking pig.

Our dining companions, a nice straight couple, were, of course, quite horrified. Who fucking wouldn't be? I was glad to note that they were as taken aback as I was by Jonny's brazen dessert pillaging. It was nice to have a unanimous expression of solidarity in the face of this kind of appalling crumble crime.

"Can you believe he snarfled my dessert?" I asked our dining companions, rhetorically.

The couple shifted uncomfortably in their chairs. The wife looked quite pained. Then the husband spoke.

"That's not why we're shocked."

So it turns out I was gravely mistaken. Yes, they were stupefied, but not by the theft of the crumble. It was the fact that I called my Jonny, the love of my life, "a fat fucking pig."

Suddenly I was in the hot seat. Instead of Jonny being under the spotlight, it was me, the innocent party, the dessert-deprived victim, who was on trial.

Our evening of fine dining was devolving into a whole Judge Judy situation. Acquittal would require a vigorous defense. I marshaled my arguments.

Firstly, I explained, Jonny is not fucking fat. It is, therefore, perfectly permissible to accuse him of being so. If he were to become fat, which is unlikely given the fact that he is a self-confessed exercise fucking bulimic, I would be far less inclined to call him a fat fucking pig. Note the phrase "less inclined." I could not give a 100 percent guarantee that I would not call him a fat fucking pig. It would all depend, not on his level of corpulence, but on the scale of the dessert theft.

I went on to explain that fat and fat humor is a leitmotif in gay male culture. Weight gain and weight loss play a central role in any gay badinage. The reason for this is obvious: Straight men spend all day long accusing each other, with varying degrees of hostility and idiocy, of being gay, acting gay, looking gay, etc. Gay men cannot really flip this trope around and accuse each other of being straight. This would be retarded. But they can grab the next biggest cultural bête noire: fat. And grab they do, regardless of how thin or fat the grabee, by the handful.

Every gay conversation is larded with fat humor.

When a gay tells another gay that he's got a new bloke on the hook, the response is quite likely to be something on the order of "So he's a chubby chaser, right?"

When a gay tells a fellow gay that he is about to go on TV or head for an important job interview and wants advice on what to wear, the response may well be "How about vertical stripes and a mask?" or something equally unhelpful but hilarious.

This relentless teasing can also be self-directed. If a gay man packs on five pounds, he is quite likely to start referring to himself as Precious. This kind of self-deprecating humor is about self-preservation. Gays are adept at giving themselves a little pinch or a tweak before a pal has the chance to do so.

Why are the gays so focused on their physicality?

Again the answer is screechingly obvious: Straight dudes are attracted to female perfection. What they look for in a female—boobs, ass, legs, etc.—they do not expect to see in themselves. They are, in fact, disastrously oblivious to their own physicality and feel no compulsion whatsoever to improve upon their own attractiveness. It's *me tubby Tarzan, you skinny hot Jane*, as far as most straights are concerned.

Gay men, like straight men, are also on the hunt for idealized bodies. But, and this is a big but, the difference is that gay men are pursuing their own gender. Since we are attracted to ourselves, we cannot very well have one set of rules for ourselves and another for the object of our affections. It has to be *you buff Tarzan and me buff Tarzan*.

Second, Jonathan is, as evidenced by the stolen crumble, definitely and indisputably, for all the world to see, an unapologetic pig. Stealing dessert is a piggish thing to do.

My defense was reaching a crescendo . . .

And, while we are on the subject, ladies and gentlemen of the jury, one must ask the question, is it so terrible to *be* a pig? Is it really insulting or defamatory to call somebody a pig? Not really. Pigs are God's creatures, just like us. And some of them are very cute. Right? Who doesn't love those little potbellied numbers?

Time for closing arguments. Time to play my trump card. As my final salvo, I drew the courtroom's attention to the fact that Jonny, the recipient of my micro-tirade, was not exactly behaving like a person who had been victimized. Far from being offended, he was amused and delighted and triumphant and fucking replete.

Despite reassurances from Jonny himself that he had no problem with this level of playful badinage, the couple remained convinced that he was deeply hurt. As a last resort I gave two additional examples of profanity-strewn insults which had recently passed between Jonathan and myself. I wanted them to see that this kind of seemingly abrasive humor was, in our lives, quite quotidian.

Me: I've had such a heinous day. Rub my feet, would you, luv?

Jonny: Rub them yourself, you toxic little dwarf.

Jonny: Our living room really needs a new rug.

Me: Well, that's the pot calling the kettle black.

This only made matters worse. Clearly there was no way to reduce the general discomfort, particularly that of the wife, so I flung my arms in the air, like I just didn't care, and embarked on another distracting anecdote.

The next day, I had a chance to regroup with the hetero male in question at the water cooler. He seemed to have recovered from the pig debacle and was anxious to chat.

"Fags are so lucky. You can say *anything* to each other."

"To what are you referring?"

"You can call each other a fat fucking pig and it's totally okay."

This time it was my turn to be horrified and perplexed.

"You mean to tell me that if you called your wife a fat fucking pig *she would actually be genuinely offended?*"

"Not only would she be offended. She would probably have me arrested and then divorce me."

"Whaaa?"

"I would end up on some dreadful list of registered wife-abusers and never be allowed to live in a respectable neighborhood again. No straight dude can ever call his girlfriend or wife a fat fucking pig."

"Not even in jest?"

"Don't you get it? Chicks are very sensitive, especially about the size of their asses, and, for that matter, about everything. We straight dudes have to tread on eggshells 24/7. Every time we open our mouths, we end up having to atone in some way or other."

"What would happen if you got carried away and it just slipped out? Fat fucking pig! Like you had Tourette's syndrome? Or what if you said, 'just kidding,' right after, you know, with oodles of sincerity."

"Even if she did not hire a hit man or divorce me, she would punish me by withholding sex and refusing to cook my favorite meals."

I looked at my colleague in a whole new, sympathetic light.

These poor earnest straight dudes! I thought they ruled the world, but clearly they are little more than shock absorbers for female rage. They grow up under the crushing influence of one woman, their mother. They then have a brief period of fabulous, self-determining, keg-guzzling nihilism in their early twenties. Then they innocently get married and—bam!—they are right back where they started. The poor little luvs.

The henpecked hetero began to catalogue the reasons why being gay was so infinitely advantageous. Sex loomed large on the list. Along with being able to insult each other with boisterous, schoolboyish impunity, gay men can also shag each other without all the folderol which it apparently takes to peel the panties off the average straight woman. The wooing, the Interflora fantasias, the accoutrements of heterosexual seduction are unimaginably elaborate and costly. While the average straight dude is wondering how many more Whitman's Samplers he will need to cough up before he gets his knob polished, the equivalent gay dude has already buffed and polished multiple knobs to a gleaming, blinding patina. While some poor hetero bloke is painstakingly penning corny love poems, after strewing his duvet with baby's breath and powdering his various private areas, his gay equivalent is already "cleaning up" after shag number seventeen.

And then there's the deranged etiquette of postcoital communications. While gay men can make assignation after assignation with brusque informality, straight women, so my straight pal assured me, demand a cavalcade of cooing texts, reassuring e-mails and solicitous phone calls after just one date.

No wonder straight men all drop dead early from stress, heart attacks and strokes!

The crumble debacle, and the follow-up convo at the water cooler, had a salutary effect on me. These incidents gave me a fresh appreciation for my gay-dom and the freedoms and advantages which cascade down on me and my co-inverts at regular intervals. As a result, I have achieved a new level of glad-to-be-gay serenity. Every day I wake up and thank the Lord I was born a happy-go-lucky, card-carrying fag.

For many gays, myself included, the emergence of a gay sensibility during childhood and adolescence is fraught with agonara.* The Sturm und Drang, the coming to terms with it all, the bullying, the mockery all make for a traumatizing experience. But then, once the self-determining years arrive, one must acknowledge that being gay is the most insane gift, the ultimate Whitman's Sampler.

The advantages of being gay are hard to put into words: I liken the experience of being a poofter to the coronation scene in Eisenstein's agonara-filled movie *Ivan the Terrible*. The tsar sits on the throne while attendants pour buckets of gold coins over his head. To be a gay man is to be anointed and showered with riches. To be a straight man, on the other hand, is to be perpetually careening toward catastrophe, down the steps of Odessa, baby carriage akimbo, in *The Battleship Potemkin*.

My straight colleague, as you no doubt noted, was, like all heterosexuals, extremely focused on matters of the flesh. His envy of gay people was largely driven by the idea that gays can rut each other's brains out whenever the mood strikes. There are, however,

---

*My friend Johnny Rozsa invented this word. Translation: extreme agony.

so many more profound nonsexual advantages to being gay than were dreamt of in his universe, Horatio.

One of my personal faves: Gays can cross socioeconomic and geographical boundaries. Having escaped from a crap town, I am living proof of this fact. All the hetero losers I grew up with are all, ironically, stuck back in Bumfuck. By the time I was twenty-one I had left them all behind and was, courtesy of the gay men I met, already mincing my way into the fabulousness of big-city life. To visit a gay bar back then was to mix with barrow boys and earls. There we were, young glam-rock Bowie fans and aging Peggy Lee fans, all pissing in the same pot. The heterosexuals of the world never get to enjoy this kind of classless, mashed-up milieu. With their dreary political affiliations and their turgid country-club memberships, they are doomed to waste their lives in a stagnant vat of turgid homogeneity.

Back to me.

By the age of twenty-five I had transcended my low beginnings, clawed my way to the middle, snagged a job in L.A. and was living in an apartment building opposite Bette Davis! This was before the screen legend had a stroke. She was still ballsy and brassy and knocking back the Scotch. *Et voilà!* A typical gay trajectory: in less than a decade you can go from living opposite the biscuit factory to living opposite Bette Davis.

More advantages. Gays are sought after. Straights stay home, while gays go out. To be gay is to be deluged with invitations to gallery openings, fashion shows and bar mitzvahs. This sounds superficial until you think about it from the straight not-invited-to-anything point of view. Then it starts to get heavy, man.

I once shared an apartment with a straight bloke. Every time the mail arrived, he had a giant mood swing, and I don't blame him. All the fun party invites were for me. My mantelpiece was full. His was empty. It was really quite poignant. Once in a while I would drag him along to some freaky fiesta or other, but this only made matters worse. Once the poor darling got a clearer sense of just how fun and fabulous all the events were that he was not being invited to, his feelings of rejection and general agonara only increased.

Gays get to self-invent in the most insanely theatrical way. We can behave in a foncy and szhooshy and fierce and fabulous way and nobody really minds. If a straight man swanned about like Karl Lagerfeld or Valentino, wafting through rooms filled with orchids, pugs and Aubusson carpets, he would be stoned to death. As gays, Val and Karl have carte blanche to lounge about, eat marrons glacés and live the lives of perfumed potentates.

Lastly and most importantly, gays get to exaggerate. The permission to embroider and hyperbolize is one of the most amazingly liberating aspects of poofterdom. While rigor and accuracy are the foundations of hetero male society, nobody in his right mind expects a gay to stick to the hard facts. While straight guys are doomed to live in a world of spreadsheet accountability, we fairies are free to flit about weaving gossamer dreams and obscuring the harsh realities of life with blankets of thistledown. Just don't steal our dessert, unless you want to be called a fat fucking pig.

The
MOST
IMPORTANT
WORD
in the
HISTORY
of
STYLE

How naff is Spencer Pratt? Are Snuggies naff? Is your hairdo naff? How about Bill O'Reilly? Is he naff? Do you wish your best girlfriend would stop wearing horribly naff shoes? Who is naffer, Kourtney or Khloe? Is your grandmother, in her tube tops and patent sling-backs, a naff embarrassment? Do you have any idea what I am talking about? Read on and you soon will.

My immersion in gay culture began when I got a job at the local department store in my hometown of Reading, in England. The whole place was crawling with poofs. Some were young, but most were what you might call "old school." They wore fluffy sweaters on the weekend. They went to Brighton or Bournemouth for their gay guesthouse holidays. Some had fought in the Second World War.

These tough old queens *d'un certain âge* had spent the majority of their gay lives being gay when it was illegal. They loved to tell stories of illicit gin parties with men dancing the fox-trot behind tightly drawn net curtains. These fabulous old inverts hailed from the era before the 1957 Wolfenden Report, which ten years later resulted in the legalization of homosexuality. For this reason they were often referred to by us younger poofs as the Pre-Wolfendens.

Most noteworthy was the fact that the Pre-Wolfendens had their very own language. A secret gay lingua. It was called Palare.

The most important word in the Palare dictionary—and quite possibly in the history of mankind—is *naff*. If you are even remotely interested in fashion and style, I can guarantee that, by the end of this chapter, you will be naffing up a storm.

But first, a little history.

Palare (pronounced *pol-are-ee*) was and is the first and only gay language. It has roots in seventeenth-century cant, the language of street criminals and carnies. Over subsequent centuries it was embellished with overtones of Romany, and a soupçon of Yiddish. From here this strange lingo minced its way into the music halls and the theater, where the gays nabbed it and made it their own, adding words and augmenting it with Cockney back slang and this and that.

Why did gays need their own language? You might ask the same question of Jews or African Americans. The fact is that beleaguered groups need to be able to express solidarity and share info about everything from politics to the effectiveness of certain moisturizers, and to do so without being detected.

Palare satisfied the gay need to be able to communicate covertly with other gays, and say things like "Vada the butch omi-polone with the bona carts." Translation: May I draw your attention to the masculine, well-endowed homosexual who has just walked into view.

Palare also gave the gays a way to retaliate against the straight world with undetectable barbs, as in "The ajax polone with the nante riah and the tragic oglefakes will shag anything in kaffies." Translation: The woman standing next to you, with the unfortunate hairdo and the lackluster eyewear, is in the habit of offering herself to a broad section of the male population.

After a week or two at that dusty department store, I acquired the basics of this language and was able to Palare with the best of them. The two most commonly used words in my burgeoning Palare vocab were *bona*, meaning "good," and *vada*, meaning "to look."

Some Palare expostulations were lengthy: "Vada my new bijou batts! Aren't they bona? Judging by the nanty expression on your eek, you think they are cod." Translation: Look at these nifty little shoes which I recently acquired! Aren't they terrific? Judging by the unpleasant expression on your face, you do not share my opinion in any way, shape or form.

Most of my Palare exchanges were short and concise: A simple "Vada . . . Bona!" was enough to draw a gay pal's attention to a desired object, be it a good-looking man, a pastry in a bakery window or a long-awaited town bus arriving just as a coiffure-destroying downpour was commencing.

Lest you be too impressed by the alacrity of my Palare absorption, let me point out the following: Back then I did not have much else going on. Since Britain was in the grip of a recession, there was nothing much happening in my department store. The mise-en-scène was very reminiscent of the BBC TV show *Are You Being Served?* where the less-than-busy sales staff while away the hours bantering with each other and straightening the merch. Customer appearances were few and far between. I spent most of the day chatting while inefficiently wielding a feather duster. The challenge of learning to speak Palare offered a much-needed antidote to the immense tedium of each day. I should probably have tackled Sanskrit while I was at it.

Secondly, it should be noted that Palare is not exactly what you might call a complex language. The Palare dictionary is more a pamphlet than a tome. Brochure, some might say. In fact, Palare may well be the world's dinkiest language.

The following is the Palare lingua in its entirety. Palare pedants will probably find some I have missed or misspelled. All I can say to them is "Bona for you, luvvie!"

AJAX • nearby (from "adjacent"?)

BASKET • the bulge of male genitals through clothes

BATTS • shoes

BIJOU • small

BOD • body

BOLD • daring

BONA • good

BUTCH • masculine; masculine lesbian

CAMP • effeminate (origin: KAMP = Known As Male Prostitute)

CAPELLO • hat

CARSEY • toilet (also spelled "khazi")

CARTS/CARTSO • penis

CHICKEN • young boy

CHARPER • search

CHARPERING OMI • policeman

COD • naff, vile

COTTAGE • public loo (particularly with reference to cottaging)

COTTAGING • having or looking for sex in a cottage

CRIMPER • hairdresser

DISH • an attractive male; buttocks

DIZZY • scatterbrained

DOLLY • pretty, nice, pleasant

DRAG • clothes, esp. women's clothes

ECAF • face (back slang)

EEK • face (abbreviation of "ecaf," Cockney back slang)

ENDS • hair

ESONG • nose

FANTABULOSA • wonderful

FEELE • child

FRUIT • queen

GELT • money

GLOSSIES • magazines

HANDBAG • money
HOOFER • dancer
JARRY • food, also "mangarie"
KAFFIES • trousers
KHAZI • toilet, also spelled "carsey"
LALLIES • legs
LATTY • room, house or flat
LILLS • hands
LILLY • police (Lilly Law)
LUPPERS • fingers
MANGARIE • food, also "jarry"
MEASURES • money
MEESE • plain, ugly (from Yiddish)
MESHIGENER • nutty, crazy, mental
METZAS • money
MINCE • walk (affectedly)
NAFF • See remainder of this chapter!
NANTI • not, no
NATIONAL HANDBAG • dole
NISHTA • nothing, no
OGLEFAKES • glasses
OGLES • eyes
OMI • man
OMI-POLONE • effeminate man, or homosexual

ONK • nose
ORBS • eyes
PALARE PIPE • telephone
PALLIASS • back (as in part of body)
PARK • give
PLATE • feet; to fellate
POLARI • chat, talk
POLONE • woman
POTS • teeth
RIAH/RIHA • hair
RIAH SHUSHER • hairdresser
SCARPER • to run off (from Italian *scappare*, to escape)
SCOTCH • leg
SHARPY • policeman
SHUSH • steal (from client)
SHUSH BAG • holdall
SHYKER/SHYCKLE • wig
SLAP • makeup
STRILLERS • piano
THEWS • thighs
TRADE • sex
TROLL • to walk about (esp. looking for trade)
VADA/VARDA • see
WILLETS • breasts

If you want to hear some full-throttle old-school Palare, shrieked at full velocity by a couple of Pre-Wolfendens, then YouTube the comic duo Julian and Sandy. These two insanely high-strung comedians would integrate Palare into their weekly skits on a popular BBC radio show entitled *Round the Horne*. My mum was a devotee and, like many Brits, developed, thanks to Julian and

Sandy, a glancing connection with this language: After listening to *Round the Horne* on a Sunday afternoon, Betty Doonan was often inclined to drag her bona lallies to the ajax park, or even to varda a stately latty or two, but only if her slap and riah were looking bona.

Where is Palare today?

Once homosexuality became legal, accepted and fabulous, the need for a secret language diminished rapidly and, by the 1980s, Palare became quite un-bona. As gays began to mainstream, Palare symbolized the most cod aspects of the gay ghetto, and was associated with gin-soaked, self-loathing Judy Garland devotees. Young, dynamic and integrated omi-polones saw no benefit to marginalizing their cute little selves with bonas and vadas. If they wanted to plonk their luppers on the strillers, they could do so without deploying a secret language.

Once in a while Palare rears its bona head. Todd Haynes integrated it into the screenplay of his nelly glam-rocker movie *Velvet Goldmine* with bona results. In the early nineties, Morrissey introduced groovy *Face* magazine-reading gays to the language on his album *Bona Drag*. The first track is entitled "Piccadilly Palare."

I still find myself Palare-ing once in a while. This usually happens when I run into older Brit pals. One does what one can to keep the Palare flame alive. I am happy to report that I have taught my Jonny—he has bona thews and a beautiful ecaf, and he designs bona objects for polones and omi-polones to tart-up their latties— to keep his ogles off other omi's carts.

Sadly I was forced to abandon the word "bona" when I first moved to the United States. When I worked at Maxfield in L.A., I would greet the arrival of a new shipment of high-fashion frocks with the word "bona!" This led to many embarrassing misunder-standings. My concerned colleagues thought I was saying "boner."

As much as I would like to see it come back, I know, sadly, that the moment has passed. Palare has gone the way of the green carnation. (Edwardian gays wore green carnations to telegraph their illegal proclivities.)

I am at peace with this. I have found a way to live in a world where nobody talks about bona ogle-riahs or cod khazis.

There is one exception, however, one vital Palare word which I will not, indeed, cannot, relinquish. In fact, I am clinging on to it for dear life.

I am talking about "naff."

"Naff" may just be the most important word in the history of history. It remains as useful and resonant today as it was when I was staring into the wrinkled eeks of those Pre-Wolfenden omi-polones and first learning to Palare all those years ago. And yet, naff remains neglected and underutilized, especially in the United States.

I have tried repeatedly to import "naff" to the States, but with-out much success. I feel that this will eventually happen. It's logical. It's inevitable. Why? Because there is a massive, bottom-less naff-shaped hole in the American dictionary.

The best current translation for "naff" is probably "a depress-ing lack of style." This was, however, not the original meaning. Hang on to your cod shyckles. Gird up your willets with bona drag. This is a good one . . .

"Naff" was originally a gay slang word used by gay men when they were out trolling. Here is a specific instance: If gay man A saw that gay man B was interested in a third man, C, and A knew that C was straight, then A might well say to B, "Don't bother vardaring his eek or his carts. He's naff." This was done by A in order to prevent B getting his eek smashed in by C, which would be hideously un-bona for B.

So what the fuck, you are no doubt screaming, did "naff" actually mean? I am glad you asked.

"Naff" was a sassy little acronym for "Not Available for Fucking," i.e., "straight," i.e., stop vardaring him, right now!

Over the years, "naff" the acronym became synonymous with all things hetero. Gradually the meaning morphed. Ere long it came to mean not just "straight" but also "dreary," i.e., un-gay, i.e., lacking in stylish savoir faire.

As I pointed out in no uncertain terms at the beginning of this book, gay men are basically Frenchwomen with penises. Like the frogettes, we believe passionately in our own connoisseurship and our stylistic superiority, and in the style inferiority of the straight world. It was, therefore, inevitable that "naff"—a word which meant "straight"—would soon come to mean "unstylish."

Who's the naff omi in the tragic shyckle?

"Naff" deserves a bigger canvas. It is a phenomenally useful word with no single-word equivalents on either side of the Atlantic. Remember, "tacky" means "cheap or glitzy," whereas "naff" is about stylistic shortcomings which are horrifyingly average and pathetically ordinary.

The Jersey Shore is tacky, but *The Bachelor* is naff.

Mariah Carey is gorgeously tacky but Celine Dion is just plain naff.

Michael Bolton is naff but Josh Groban is mega-naff.

John Edwards is tacky but John Boehner is naff.

While useful for critiquing all aspects of culture, naff is most useful when applied to fashion and style. Grab it, treasure it and use it to death. After all, you live in a world where fashion and style have become paramount. And yet you have no word to succinctly identify an absence of either. "Naff" to the rescue.

Cultivate a nose for naff. Put it up where it belongs. Let naff guide you through all your fashion purchases. Let naff help you through a major deaccession of your appallingly naff closet. Go through all of your clothing and toss out all the naff leftovers. Treat yourself to a naff fashion enema.

Gather up all your bedazzled denim and give it to the naff broad down the street.

Give those naff white shutter-shades—the ones Kanye West wore back in the day—to your local homeless person.

Make a play tent for your naff kids out of your old, naff, over-sized eighties dropped-waist sleeveless denim dress.

Take that naff banana clip that you have been using to scrunch up your tressy riah and clip it onto the dog's tail.

Toss out those naff squishy pink Reeboks. (At the time of writing, New Balance is groovier and Nike is perfectly acceptable. Caution: This could change.)

Pour lighter fluid onto your boyfriend's ultra-naff pleated Dockers and make dusters out of his golf shirts, the uber-naff ones with the company logos.

Take all those horrible, naff, solid-peach-colored towels in your bathroom and go get some bona new Pucci-print numbers.

And that naff butterfly tramp-stamp, please cover it up with a dollop of bona slap!

CAN I
MEASURE
YOUR
INSIDE
LEG?

The twenty-first century is shaping up to be, at least from the point of view of women's fashion, the most terrifying, titillating, tumultuous, fabulously tacky, gloriously glam-obsessed, spray-tanned, deliciously deranged and relentlessly entertaining period in the history of La Mode. From Uggs to Gaga, from Lanvin to Louboutin, from Harajuku girls to porno-chic, from prepubescent Internet wundersluts to geriatric goth-ettes, the cacophony of conflicting trends, incomprehensible bloggings, narcissistic naggings and maniacal "must-have" musings is only getting louder.

This confusion and mayhem has also infected the world of men's style, turning it into a chemically volatile miasma of sartorial confusion. Today's lumberjack is tomorrow's lounge lizard. Today's peacock is tomorrow's feather duster. Tomorrow's feather duster will be next week's Lady Gaga chapeau. In other words, all the old rules are crumbling, everything is kookoo and heterosexual men have no idea what to wear.

Straight dudes have always been fucked up when it comes to

dressing. For every Cary Grant or James Dean there have always been eight million hastily assembled schlumps dressed head to foot in unironically crumpled moderate sportswear. You, the straight men of the world, are a *shonda* of biblical proportions. Most of you are so randomly attired that you make Chris Farley look like the Duke of Windsor. Most of you are so ratty you make Ratso Rizzo look like Nacho Figueras. Most of you are so unprepossessing you make Buddy Hackett look like Joan Hackett.

The reasons for this should be addressed in order that the healing can begin. Let's start with that gruesome archive of dress shirts.

Straight guys are dress-shirt hoarders. There is no room for anything groovy in those stag closets because they are completely stuffed with miles of dreary striped business shirts. Their lack of fashion savoir faire renders these guys incapable of determining that a particular shirt has had its day and needs to be given to the Goodwill. Anything new is added to that endless, dismal Chinese laundry of an archive. No sorting or deaccessioning ever takes place. Nice new shirts are mixed in with tragic ancient shirts with rotting green-hued armpits.

Adding to the coagulation is the fact that straight guys constantly receive new dress shirts as holiday or birthday gifts. Because they are essentially very easygoing—I often think of straight guys as Labrador dogs—they never object to such a less-than-sizzling *cadeau*. Such is not the case with gay men: Any self-respecting homo would be outraged and shocked if another gay man gave him something as horribly *useful* and quotidian as a business shirt. It's the equivalent of buying Mum a new frying pan on Mother's Day.

Sidebar. The thought of receiving a dress shirt for my birthday sends me lurching for the Kevorkian euthanasia kit. If you are thinking about buying a gift for me, or for any gay man, here are some examples of the kind of stuff which might hit the spot: a gift certificate for a massage administered by the European soccer star of my choice; a massive monogrammed white Goyard steamer trunk containing a little *quelque chose d'autre*; an invitation to ride with the grand marshal of the annual Coney Island Mermaid Parade and/or New York Puerto Rican Day Parade.

Back to shirts, and the reasons why straight men might have such a monstrous and fetid inventory thereof.

The final reason many straight men overload on shirts? Many guys—the poor deluded darlings!—are suffering from a Gatsby complex. Remember that scene in *The Great Gatsby* where the hero of the title, played by a pornographically young and handsome Robert Redford, flings his Turnbull & Asser collection around the room? It is almost as if he is ejaculating men's shirts all over Daisy, played by Mia Farrow. He only stops when she starts to weep at the sheer virile beauty and abundance of all those flying garments. In this scene, Gatsby's shirt collection symbolizes everything a straight dude craves: enigma, power and a wilting, fawning female. This Redford moment has left its mark on generations of straights: *I'll get a bunch of shirts and maybe the rest will follow* is how they interpret it.

Guess what? You are not the Great Gatsby. Now, take every dress shirt which is over five years old and fling it, Gatsby-style, out of your bedroom window. There's a good boy!

Now let's talk ties.

According to Sigmund Freud, neckties are phallic symbols.

This makes perfect sense to me, as exemplified by the fact that, in the uptight fifties, tie styles became incredibly pinched and narrow. During the free-love, androgynous, far-out hippie years, they disappeared completely from the necks of young men. By the time the hedonistic, swinging, gonorrhea-riddled seventies rolled around, ties had become obscenely oversize, thick and priapic.

Many gay men now eschew a tie in preference for a more interesting belt. Thus, the emphasis is shifting from the face to the nether regions. If we are to follow the teachings of Freud literally, then this is the equivalent of removing your penis from your neck, where it had the potential to throttle you, and tying it around your waist. This seems, upon reflection, either a great idea or a terrible waste of a penis, but doing so does get it back in the general area where it belongs.

All right already with the amateur psychobabble. Straight men are confused enough as it is. It's time for some much-needed solutions.

The current fashion apocalypse has rendered straight men even more fashion phobic than before. What was once merely bewildering is now mind-numbingly off-putting. So how should a straight dude attempt to navigate this endless sea of options and styles?

Follow the gay with the red balloon.

You straight dudes are best served by trailing us gays. We have your best interests at heart. Our goal is to simplify, demystify and defang the world of fashion for you so that you can enjoy the process of adornment just like everyone else, and, most important, look like less of a schlub.

Paging all straight dudes: there are three key men's designer fashion trends which were jump-started by the gays but which work well for dudes of all persuasions. Yes, these trends are ambidextrous. They represent a long overdue entente cordiale between gay style and straight lack thereof. It's time to merge. It's time to relax and sparkle.

Regarding matters of style, I have, as previously stated, no desire to transform the straight men of the world into screaming, scented label-queens, even though it would obviously be quite amusing to do so. But if, after heeding my advice and exhortations, you straight blokes could just gussy yourselves up even just a tad, we gays would be hugely grateful, and so would your long-suffering girlfriends and wives.

Don't worry, dudes: There are no sequined jockstraps or over-the-shoulder boulder holders. I have deliberately avoided anything which might be deemed "too gay." The selected styles are guaranteed not to jeopardize your perceived virility in any way. In some instances my recommendations may even enhance it.

Whether you are gay or straight, or a gal who is just looking for a simple way to de-schlump her boyfriend, or a femme lesbian who is trying to natty up her frowzy stone-butch girlfriend, you will find salvation in my tristate solution.

Breeze through the following three concepts and circle back on the one which best resonates with your particular brand of masculinity. If you cannot decide, then grab a gay and garner his input.

THE PERVERSE PREP

Who doesn't want to look like a tight-assed congressman from the early 1960s?

This arch and intriguing movement was started in the mid '00s by younger gays who began experimenting with an insanely hyperconventional look. It's a perverse parody of archconservative, straight Waspy style. It's Ralph Lauren squared.

A neat gray Thom Browne or Band of Outsiders shrunken suit is the basic requirement. Skinny flat-front ankle-revealing pants end about three inches above heavy wingtip shoes. Bare ankles are revealed. Since the carrying of an umbrella is much too self-indulgent and Mr. Farnsworth-ian for this pared-down look, a simple beige knee-length raincoat protects the wearer from any precipitation. It's a look that screams, "IBM circa 1958," or, at the very least, "I'm a fresh-faced Jehovah's Witness!"

Codified accessories play a key role in the Perverse Prep look: dorky, heavy-framed spectacles; skinny knit ties with tie clips, or bow ties; aluminum briefcases and scrupulously ironed white linen handkerchiefs. It's all very Gilbert & George.

As you saw during Operation Goldilocks, we gays love to take straight looks and parody them. The Perverse Prep, with its emphatically hetero roots, is a great example of straight-style theft. For the gay, it was a hip, irony-drenched moment. For the late-adopter hetero stag in search of a little style, it's a look which exudes restrained stylish competence. Finally, you, Mr. Straight Stuff, are wearing a suit which fits.

Let's talk about *fit*.

Listen up, straight dudes: A suit is an organizing principle. The whole raison d'être of a suit is to give you an aura of capability and gravitas and to give your body a more defined shape. In order to do that, a suit must have more than a glancing connection to your body. It must fit. This basic point seems to have eluded straight men. They are terrified that anything should feminize their bodies. As a result, straight guys, in their atrociously boxy jackets with appalling baggy pants, resemble the fat detectives on *The Wire*.

This inclination toward oversized, flapping garments reflects a primitive and obsolete desire to look big and terrifying. It's the same impulse which causes straight men to puff up their chests and walk with their hands turned out, à la George Bush. Look at me. I am such a gorilla. Aren't you scared?

Heed well the words of the ranting homosexual. He is not here to drag you out of your comfort zone and turn you into the office peacock. He just wants you *not* to look like a Belushi. Submit to the fit. Forget about that poofy old Gatsby, because now you are Steve McQueen in *The Thomas Crown Affair*.

Now let's talk about black.

If the gray Perverse Prep suit is a little too perverse and Orwellian for you, then I suggest you try black.

Caution: Black will make you appear less competent and diminish your chances of promotion. However, a nifty, spiffy black suit will make up for any loss of boardroom credibility by giving you a Rat Pack sizzle. In other words: you will get shagged more often.

I am a huge Rat Pack devotee. Whether you are a gay or straight, a sharp black suit will always add a little hedonistic sizzle to your life. It's also a fantastic choice for a skinny stone-butch lesbian. (Hefty stone-butch lesbians should avoid it, unless they have a specific desire to look like Winston Churchill.)

For many years I have proudly owned one of Sammy Davis Junior's original shirts. It was a super-sleazy ruffled number made by the original Rat Pack shirtmaker, Nat Wise of Beverly Hills. The style—high collared and tailless with mini side-vents worn outside the pants—was called The Lady's Man. This shirt was clearly designed to be worn by Sammy during the execution of a fast-paced stage show. Like most gays, I have always dreamed of having my very own fast-paced stage show. I want to sweat and slide from one end of the stage to the other, milking the adoration, bathing in that pink spotlight and cradling the audience in the palm of my hand. Wearing this shirt is about as close as I will ever get.

Despite my adoration for Sammy, I fully recognize that the Rat Pack was a club I could never have joined. If I had so much as tried to insert my fast-paced gay self into their testosterone-drenched milieu, Sammy and Dean and Frank would have kicked my gay ass all the way over to Liberace's house. My Rat Pack affectation is merely an affectionate fuck-you to those coked-out homophobes.

So there you have it. The Perverse Prep gray suit, or, if that particular style martini is too dry for y'all, then rock it in black and start channeling Sammy D.

THE DOUCHE BAG LOOK

I am an equal opportunity gay. I feel that both gay and straight men have the right to be flashy, nouveau riche, nouveau poor and tacky. I also feel that "good taste" is an illusion, a subjective instrument of oppression which prevents people from expressing themselves. Fashion is a jigsaw puzzle, and without the glorious tackiness there can be no nifty preppiness.

Popularized by the cast members of *Jersey Shore*, the Douche Bag look is the polar opposite of the Perverse Prep. I for one am a huge fan. Here's why: I love it because it's brave, flamboyant and wildly unpretentious. Welcome to the world of Ed Hardy.

Permit me to explain: Ed Hardy, for those of you who have not turned on your TV since *Roseanne* was the top-rated show, is a fabulously gaudy fashion phenomenon created by designer Christian Audigier. Whether you know the name or not, you have seen the designs a million times: Those signature tattoo-inspired T-shirts—Death Before Dishonor, or Love Kills Slowly—and bedazzled accoutrements are a staple of reality shows of the *Rock of Love* genre. The depressed husband on *Jon & Kate Plus 8* was known for rocking a ferocious tiger-embellished Ed Hardy T-shirt.

The dotted line to reality TV, *Jersey Shore* in particular, has not only made Ed Hardy hugely successful, it has also made it the bête noire of the fashion cognoscenti. A veritable synonym for "bad taste." The hipsters of today who wear Margiela and tote Alexander Wang vest bags would rather jump in a lake of boiling cheddar than adorn themselves with cheesy Ed Hardy–ware.

At the time of writing, Abercrombie & Fitch execs are offering The Situation money to stop wearing their duds on the show. Clearly they are terrified of becoming mashed up with items from his Ed Hardy collection. As I scribble these very words, CNN is calling. They want me to comment on the Abercrombie-Situation situation.

Why me?

Once in a while, in the course of my style scribblings for the *New York Observer* and then Slate.com, I nabbed a scoop. Such was the case in 2010 when I broke the story on Snookie's switch from Coach to Gucci.

So, remember how Snookie, drunk or sober, was never seen without that Coach bag dangling from the crook of her arm? Snookie and her Coach were as synonymous as the Sitch and his six-pack. But then the winds of change started blowing on *The Jersey Shore*. Every photograph of guido-huntin' Snookie showed her toting a new designer purse. Why the sudden disloyalty? Was she trading up? Was she vomiting into her purses and then randomly replacing them? The answer is much more intriguing.

Allegedly, the anxious folks at these various luxury houses are all aggressively gifting our gal Snookums with free bags. No surprise, right? But here's the shocker: They are not sending her their *own* bags. *They are sending her one another's bags! Competitor's bags!*

Call it what you will: "Preemptive product placement"? "Unbranding"? Either way it's devious and wicked.

As the Snookstress odyssey continues, it will be interesting to watch her bag evolution. What will happen next? Will Gucci send her a truckload of Goyard? Will Goyard then deluge her with

Valextra? (If Snookie starts carrying a Valextra bag, it is inevitable that she will malaprop the name into Valtrex. This will doubtless accelerate the inevitable preemptive strike by Casa Valextra.)

Separately, Snookie's meteoric and lucrative ascent means that she will soon be able to sidestep the whole issue and buy her own Birkin, thereby precipitating a mass suicide over at Maison Hermès. (Warning! Hermès can easily be Snookie-spoken into Herpes.)

I feel a certain solidarity with Snookie, and not just because we are both four feet nine inches tall: I too have been a pawn/victim of preemptive product placement. Let me explain: For a number of years now I have been a loyal devotee of the Gucci shoe. They are comfy and classy and the commitment to prominent logo placement appeals to my unapologetic nouveau riche sensibility.

Whenever possible, I purchase these sneakers and slip-ons at Barneys, enjoying as I do, after over twenty-five years of loyal service, an anesthetizing discount. However, being small of foot, I am often forced to patronize a Gucci flagship in order to acquire the requisite size. Earlier this year, following a series of full-retail purchases at the Fifth Avenue store, I took it into my head to request, by repeated e-mail, a "press discount." These attempts have been totally unsuccessful: no discount has been forthcoming. When rumors began to fly regarding Snookie's purses, it suddenly occurred to me that I was in the same boat as the reality megastar: the Gucci folks would clearly prefer to discourage my loyalty rather than foster it. Snookie and I are the Typhoid Marys of the luxury-branding world.

Oh! There's the doorbell! Must dash! It's probably a FedEx

package of Crocs—anonymously sent by Gucci—in a desperate attempt to release my brand-corroding death grip on their sacred image.

The bottom line: most fashion people pull out a crucifix at the very mention of the names *Jersey Shore* or Ed Hardy.

I am not "most fashion people." I defend Monsieur Audigier. I defend America's right to be tacky. The colorful polyester Nik Nik shirts and tight pants of the disco seventies—remember Travolta and his pals in *Saturday Night Fever?*—were similarly attacked. Criticizing the Sitch or Ed Hardy for being in bad taste is like saying that Elvis was flashy or that Liberace was tacky. It's a giant case of DUH! Of course it's cheesy! That's the whole point, you doo-doo heads. Ed Hardy is hedonistic, naughty and badass and, the ultimate crime in the world of haute fashion, Ed Hardy is *fun*!

Ultimately it's a class thing: at one end of the spectrum we have the Duke of Windsor, the ultimate Waspy Ralph Lauren–esque icon of old-money taste and restraint, and at the other we have—cue the fist-bumping, pounding anthemic dance tracks—The Sitch! Lowbrow, low class and utterly without pretension, and, of course, me, the Duke of Windows, in my Sammy Davis shirts.

Instead of knocking the Douche Bag look, the style arbiters of the world should be grateful. Monsieur Audigier has done a real mitzvah to the insecure fashion insiders: he has given them something about which to feel superior. If Ed Hardy did not exist, they would have to invent it in order to get their snooty fix.

To those fashion elitists who inveigh against the Douche Bag look, I say this: remember what the great oracle Diana Vreeland said on the subject. "A little bad taste is like a nice splash of paprika. We all need a splash of bad taste—it's hearty, it's healthy, it's physical. No taste is what I'm against."

So if you, like Ronnie and Vinny and Pauly D, favor bold, flashy T-shirts with gaudy Goth embellishments or tattoo-inspired graphics, then go for it. Gay or straight or guido, this is the life-is-for-living-so-screw-the-oppressive-notion-of-good-taste look for you.

At the end of the day isn't it better to wear a tattoo T-shirt than get a real tattoo? At least you can take it off when you are obliged to undergo an embarrassing in- or out-patient procedure, wart removal and the like.

THE HERITAGE HENRY LOOK

The Heritage Henry offers both straight and gay men an unimpeachably butch way to build a casual wardrobe. I'm talking carpenter pants, cotton Amish-style jackets, collarless cotton grandpa shirts and Depression-era work boots.

Here's the deal: In the last few years we have seen various American work-wear brands leap forth from obscurity and reinvent themselves: Carhartt, Dickies, Woolrich, Filson and so many more. The resulting Heritage Henry clothing is honest and earnest and makes the wearer appear as if he belongs in a Dorothea Lange photograph.

The Heritage Henry is very popular. Suddenly there is a lemminglike rush back to a time when people raised their own chickens, yanked out one another's teeth with rusty pliers and made their own toilet paper, aka my childhood.

Instead of throwing on a sharp suit and heading to Wall Street, motivated young dudes with waxed moustaches are now throwing on canvas work duds and making organic pickles.

The fabulous irony of all this Depression-era fetishization is particularly piquant for moi. My mother, Betty, left school at the age of thirteen in rural Northern Ireland and was sent to work with a pork butcher. As she hacked off the trotters and ears of the unwittingly organic animals, she dreamed of the day when she could tear off her authentic work wear, escape to the big city, bleach her hair, wear nylons, drink gin cocktails and never step in animal feces again. She would have been very amused, as am I, to see people at the apex of urban glamour donning heritage aprons and willingly, ardently, passionately and enthusiastically electing to earn their living by deep-frying artisanal doughnuts in hand-harvested pig lard.

As unwittingly hilarious as the heritage/authenticity movement is, it has also created a solid sartorial opportunity for straights and gays alike. Here, finally, is a way for you to be stylish and au courant while radically increasing your butch factor. The authentic work pants, sturdy bib overalls, indestructible calico shirts, and undyed organic wool henleys are the ne plus ultra of unimpeachable masculinity. Heritage wear, with its evocations of ranching, railway building and pioneering spirit, *is* masculinity.

Caution: If you have a lisp, plucked eyebrows or any supernelly, Proustian affectations, such as smoking through a pink coral cigarette holder or marcel waving your hair, you may wish to avoid this earnest style. Try the Perverse Prep instead.

So there we have it: the Douche Bag, the Perverse Prep and the Heritage Henry. Take your pick. Pick a finger.

Are you a fist bumper, a pickle maker, or the man in the gray flannel suit? Choose now or forever wander the bleak and confusing landscape of the fashion apocalypse.

Bonne chance!

MOOBS
and
FAT
ASSES

Straight men have moobs. Gay men don't.

Whether it's poolside in Palm Beach or jiggling down a water-slide in Las Vegas, those soft, squishy, unappetizing, hairy man-hooters are everywhere. And, grab your man bras, because they are only becoming more pendulous, more ample and more ubiquitous.

Nobody likes a man boob. There are no fetish clubs for moob-sters or moob chasers. Moobs serve no useful purpose and the world would be an infinitely better place if they were eradicated. In this regard, they are like cockroaches, toenail fungus, mosqui-toes or stinging jellyfish. (Coincidentally, some of the pale, trans-lucent moobs actually resemble jellyfish.) In other words, moobs are a pointless blight on our otherwise beautiful planet.

Unfortunately, the majority of moobers are reluctant to even admit that there is a problem. They flaunt their pendulous moot-ers with nary a backward glance. How do we create self-awareness in those recalcitrant dudes who flaunt their floppy, milkless man hooters with no regard for the horror they are inflicting on the rest of us? There has to be a way of stemming this tidal wave of jiggling appendages. As Maureen McGovern so eloquently put it, "There's got to be a morning after."

There is hope for moob-kind: Surgical moob removal has now become a significant new growth area—if you'll pardon the expression—for plastic surgeons. I hear it's even giving vaginal rejuvenation a run for its money. But here's the rub: while a surgical moobectomy will remove the offense, it does not guarantee against future moobage. Unless Cliff and Morty start hitting the gym, those ugly suckers will just grow back.

The gym. The gym. The gym! Get your jiggly, wobbly self to the gym, you lazy punk-ass bitches.

Here's the deal: The mooblessness of gay men is entirely and utterly and simply attributable to their gym addiction. Straight guys, with the exception of the Guido Steroid Gorilla genre, rarely share this addiction. *Et voilà!* Man boobs!

This, by the way, is a complete reversal of the typical high school scenario where the soft, squishy, pale, limp-wristed gays while away the hours needle-pointing and playing badminton, and the rock-hard, pec-perfect, Abercrombie, just stepped-right-out-of-a-Bruce-Weber-photo-shoot, strapping hetero jocks are the ones with the unimpeachable physiques. Then comes the big switch-eroo. Once adulthood arrives—BAM!—everything does a total 180: the straights get fat and the gays get ab-fabulous.

Despite the disintegration of his former godlike fabulousness, the straight dude continues to play images of his old pectastic self in his head. He becomes a regional sales manager. He buys a Hyundai. He moobs up. When he squeezes himself into a booth at his local Arby's, he blithely plonks his man boobs on the Formica tabletop and banters with the waitress, his former prom date. Sheesh! He cannot believe how that gal has let herself go.

Back to the problem at hand: How can we motivate these former-football-gods-turned-squishy? What will it take to get these moobers and shakers to join a gym?

If we can analyze the motivations of gay gym-addicted men, maybe we can identify and isolate a moob motivator which can be dangled in front of the straight dudes.

Reason number one why gay men love the gym: shits and giggles. For many gay men, the gym is a place of chuckle-filled social interaction. Rather than a place of punishment, the gym is regarded with warmth and affection. A second home.

Gay men become so attached to their gyms that they invent affectionate nicknames for them. Here are a few examples from the New York City area:

Better Bodies = Bitter Beauties

David Barton = Dolly Parton

American Fitness = Mary Can You Lift This?

The Printing House = The Primping House

Pumping Iron = Pumping Irene

New York Health and Racquet Club = New York Help Me Whack It Club

How can Mr. Straight Stuff develop this kind of jolly, kicky attitude toward his gym? How might we get him to the point where he pops in, à la *Cheers*, and finds a place where everyone actually does know his stupid name?

There is only one way: start serving alcohol.

Let's put this somewhat reckless idea on hold for a moment and continue with our exploration.

Next reason: Gay men go to the gym more often than straight dudes because homos have more *me* time. To be gay is to live a life of fabulous, perfumed, szhooshy, bonbon-nibbling self-involvement. With our fancy vacations, our flower arrangements, seated lunches, and massages, we resemble those brittle, cunty, selfish, pampered socialites from the 1950s. If we don't have the time to skip off to Bitter Beauties or the Primping House, then who does?

Straight dudes, on the other hand, live in an obligation-encrusted maelstrom of self-denial. They all suffer from underarm BO because they have no time to even slap on the Mitchum, never mind bathe. The *me* time of the average heterosexual male is consumed with soul-destroying, mind-numbing commitments like mowing the lawn, helping the kids with their homework and changing Granny's colostomy bag.

Every now and again a straight bloke gets handed a swath of empty *me* time. Maybe Granny finally croaks or maybe the kids get kidnapped. Either way, Dad finally has time for himself. Does he rush to the gym? No. He collapses onto the couch and fritters away the hours watching sports, drinking kegs of beer and eating something ghastly like pumpkin cheddar waffles. This is a disaster and results in something almost as gnarly as moobs: a fat ass.

If this regimen is allowed to continue, the results can be catastrophic. Those massive buttocks, combined with the moobs, gives the average straight dude the appearance of a pre-Columbian (female) fertility doll. This is not a good thing. People might respect a pre-Columbian (female) fertility doll in the context of a museum. Nobody wants to see this kind of anthropological shit happening for real.

And here's a cautionary note to any gays who are reading this and feeling all haughty and skinny and superior. Wipe that smug look off your face and listen up: As more and more of you poofters relinquish your *me* time to create traditional families, you too are horribly at risk for pre-Columbian (female) fertility doll syndrome. Moobs and fat asses can and will spread to the gay community. Abandon your gym addiction and you too will become a big mamma jamma.

Finally we come to the elephant in the room. This is the lord king bufu motivating factor which has gays all over the globe rushing to the gym as if from a burning building: I'm talking about *nudity*!

Let's bottom line it: gay men hit the gym with such exemplary ferocity because, at the gym, they get to ogle naked and partially clad individuals of the same sex.

All over the world gay men are cruising and schvitzing and flitting around those weight rooms and butt-busting benches. They take full advantage of those sweaty oops-my-towel-slipped locker-room situations. And they engage in flirtatious behaviors which often culminate in fevered mutual frottage.

The nickname for the original NYC Chelsea Gym?

Gorillas in the Mist.

Hello!

At the very least, gay men use the gym to make assignations with the intention of future frottage and copulage. Always remember that, at the end of the day, gay men are *men* and as such are subject to spontaneous libidinal explosions and other piglike occurrences.

If straight men had this kind of sassy, sexy incentive to hit the weights, there would be no more moobs. If dudes could sit in the steam room and stare at, and maybe even touch, naked women, then the gym would be their favorite place on earth. They would be working out so often that their wives and families would barely even recognize them anymore.

"Just popping out to the gym, honey!"

"What did you say your name was?"

Let's recap our three gay gym motivators and see if any can be extrapolated to motivate the moobers. Our options are as follows:

1) Install a bar.

Pro: The sale of liquor would enhance gym profitability.

Con: The bar might get the dudes into the gym foyer—*Cheers* again!—but getting them out of the bar and into the weight room creates a whole new set of problems.

2) Give straight dudes more *me* time.

Pro: Beleaguered breadwinners deserve a little pampering.

Con: There is no guarantee they will use this free time to head to the gym. More likely they will take up something pathetic like NASCAR. The result: More pre-Columbian dollitis.

3) Pay hordes of hookers to flaunt themselves at various strategic locations throughout the gym.

Pro: This would totally do the trick.

Con: Turning every gym into a cheesy swinger sitch would eliminate moobs, but it would also result in the complete disintegration of the family unit, and society would devolve into a tawdry updated Ancient Roman orgiastic hellhole. Every dude would turn into a moobless but herpes-ridden sexaholic.

So now we are back to square one. And the moobs are multiplying. What to do?

I do have one other idea up my sleeve.

It's crazy. It's a little random, but it just might work.

Here goes: Let's bring back old-fashioned eighties aerobics. I'm talking toweling headbands. I'm talking Reeboks. I'm talking scrunch socks and leg warmers. I'm talking Olivia Newton-John belting out "Let's get physical."

Let's dial back:

When I first moved to L.A., I lived in a seedy West Hollywood motel named The Tropicana. My room was directly over the legendary Duke's Coffee Shop. As a result, all of my clothing smelled like tuna melts. This did not bother me. In fact, I loved it. I was very feral. Having come directly from punk London circa 1978, I was going through a Sid and Nancy phase. I loved the scummy Tropicana pool with its ripped AstroTurf and rusted lawn furniture. I was a gritty gay.

From my window, I had a perfect view of the gym opposite. It was called The Sports Connection. (No prizes for guessing the local nickname: The Sports Erection.) I would watch the people coming and going and think hostile punk-rock thoughts about them: "Just look at all those brainless Barbie and Ken dolls! What a bunch of wankers!"

Fast-forward three years.

There I am bouncing around the mauve carpet of The Sports Connection aerobics studio wearing fluorescent leopard tights and a loose tank, with no vestige of my former punk cred.

In my defense I must say that I am not the first person to arrive in Hollywood filled with hopes and dreams, and then end up taking a severely naff nosedive. Los Angeles has a strange and transformative effect on people. You arrive in a gray flannel skirt clutching your Bryn Mawr degree, three months later you're modeling lingerie or managing a Hofbrau restaurant and wearing your hair in headphone pigtails.

In L.A. all bets are off.

Move to Hollywood and you can, quickly and without any warning, become your most tragic and cheesy self. You might think of yourself as fully formed and self-actualized, but relocate to L.A.

and suddenly you take up clogging, or you start playing the gypsy violin, or suddenly you decide to get a foxtail tattooed on your back, suggesting that Mr. Fox has gone to earth where the sun don't shine. Yes, L.A. can really ping you off in a strange and unexpected direction.

With me it was aerobics.

Skipping about in a leotard in time to cheesy music? What's not to love? I was so addicted to the endorphins that I often used to hit the gym twice a day. I loved the pull-downs the most. (Who doesn't?) I whooped through the high kicks. I hollered as I can-canned. I whimpered though my leg lifts: ". . . and six and seven and eight . . . ahhhh!" I shvitzed and clapped and *yesss*ed through the cooldowns. I even groaned happily through those insane "go for the burn," extended, revolving arm movements which were supposed to tone flabby, wobbly triceps. And I loved every naff minute of it.

Something about dancing around the huge mirrored room in unison with hordes of other naffsters touched my soul. The ensemble choreography—two hundred losers in Lycra all performing the exact same movements—triggered all kinds of cinematic fantasies. Suddenly I was Ruby Keeler, tap dancing her brains out in the chorus of a Busby Berkeley movie. Then I was George Chakiris in *West Side Story*, slicing across that mauve carpet on my way to a rumble. Then I was a Bob Fosse chorine, arching my back on all fours, obscenely, like the painted grotesques in *Cabaret*.

Speaking of cinematic delusions: The highlight of my aerobic years was the lensing of the movie *Perfect*. John Travolta and Jamie Lee Curtis were the stars. They shot the aerobics scenes at The Sports Connection in full view of us members, and wee members, like me. (My editor told me I'm allowed to make that joke twice in this book, but no more. That was number two, if I'm not mistaken.) We S.C. members were all encouraged to sign up and play background extras in the movie. It is one of the great regrets of my life—quite possibly the only regret—that I did not throw my dance belt into the ring, and give it a whirl. How fabulous to have played a role in one of the cheesiest movies in the history of cinema!

So what has all this got to do with motivating straight men to go to the gym and rid themselves of their moobs?

Perfect, as you will no doubt recall, was a very steamy, very heterosexual movie: *Hot Hetero Lycra Love* might have been a more appropriate title. Most of Travolta's scenes consist of him bumping and grinding while staring lasciviously at Jamie Lee. It really was The Sports Erection.

This was by no means an inaccurate depiction of the aerobics era: horny straight dudes were a huge part of the mauve carpet community. They even wore leg warmers! Hard to imagine, I know, but trust me, I was there, and I saw it with my very own eyes, peeking out from under my very own toweling headband. Straight guys, while avowedly ignoring us gays, sincerely enjoyed the hot, moist proximity with attractive well-toned women. What easier way to meet a nice-looking Lycra-clad lass than when you are sprawled right next to each other, counting out your leg lifts in that pose that Jane Fonda always struck on the covers of her videotapes.

There was no shortage of hot broads at The Sports Connection. Every actress-slash-model in Hollywood was toning and twirling on that mauve carpet. Celebs too. Madonna and Brooke Shields were intermittent attendees. Summertime and the hooking up was easy, breezy CoverGirl! And nobody wore distracting headphones back then. It truly was a shared, transcendent, disco hookup experience. If a straight dude spotted an alluring young lady, all he had to do was take his business card out of his teal fanny pack and slide it into her hot-pink fanny pack.

So why did aerobics die? Why did it go the way of Ton Sur Ton blousons, pet rocks, the DeLorean and *Hill Street Blues*?

It got complicated, that's why.

Eventually aerobics morphed into Jazzercise. Suddenly those simple steps, that predictable routine, became a hellishly complicated Broadway bar mitzvah. It was all fine and dandy when the routine was unvarying, and you could do it with your eyes closed. Then came Jazzercise and snazzercise and then spazzercise. Every time I hit the mauve carpet, some new zippy components had been added to the menu. I went from feeling competent and totally Olga Korbut to fumbling and tumbling.

The hetero dudes were the first to quit. No straight guy was going to subject himself to the public humiliation of blundering through a new routine in front of some hot chick.

So, let's bring it back old-school! Revive the pull-down! Go for the burn! Grab your leg warmers! Cue the Pointer Sisters' "Jump," cue that excruciating disco version of *Cats*. So what if it is the epitome of naff: at least you get to meet hot chicks.

Come on, boys!

Jiggle that pre-Columbian bootay!

Unbuckle your bulging fanny pack and let's sweat away those mooters!

The
FIRST
ELF

On two separate occasions, once while addressing matters of style and once regarding career, I have cautioned you, dear reader, against a reliance on external validation. Like for us gays, your ultimate challenge is to become approval-oblivious. Yes, this fundamental tenet of gay happiness also applies to y'all. If you can immunize yourself against both flattery and mockery, then my work will be done, and you will be free. Needlepoint *that*!

Speaking of needlepoint . . .

Years ago, back when fax machines were hip and glamorous, I faxed a handwritten missive to Oprah asking whether her fans had ever sent her tribute gifts, or "fan art." I told her that I was interested in creating a window at the Barneys in Chicago dedicated to her. In my mind I imagined the walls lined with a multitude of Oprah portraits in diverse styles, all created by her adoring fans. I got the idea when I worked on the Christie's Marilyn sale: M.M.'s fans had sent her a steady flow of corny-but-sweet crafty tributes.

As an ensemble installation, they made for an impactful and touching visual.

Oprah's assistant faxed back and told me to head on over to Harpo Productions tout de suite.

I naturally expected a minion would be accompanying me to some kind of cavernous warehouse. Instead it was Oprah herself. She flung open the door of the giant storage facility, declaring, in her signature full-volume baritone, "FAN ART!"

And there it was, as far as the eye could see, a veritable Walmart of FAN ART! A Kmart of crafty creations, sploggy oil portraits, kooky collages, nifty needlepoints, crocheted Oprah effigies, Oprah in bargello, Oprah mosaics, Oprah. Oprah. Oprah, as far as the eye could see, OPRAH! (Baritone.)

As I examined these poignant, heartfelt homages to the fabulous queen of all media, I found myself getting unexpectedly emotional. Here was the ultimate healing therapy for Oprah's hardscrabble childhood. I had not cried in a while. It was strange that it took Oprah's avalanche of FAN ART! to get the waterworks going.

"This is all so beautiful and touching," I said, clutching a glitter-strewn gouache of Oprah as the Statue of Liberty.

"Yes it's true," said Oprah, sighing philosophically, "but keep in mind that many of these lovely objects are sent to me with"—signature Oprah pause—"INVOICES!"

The moral of the story: external adulation can fill an emotional void, but it may come at a price, literally.

Continuing the warehouse theme . . .

There is a huge, nondescript storage facility located about a half hour from the center of Washington, D.C. It houses all the holiday decorations from presidential administrations past. To poke through this twinkly archive is to examine U.S. history. Here lie giant spools of Nancy Reagan's favorite red ribbon, as lush and thick as the shoulder pads on an Adolfo socialite suit. What's in that crate? Oh look, Pat Nixon's beautiful glass balls, beaded and stitched with Fabergé-esque anal retention. Not everything in the warehouse is labeled. It's fun to rummage and play guess-the-First-Lady. From chic hand-painted Venetian baubles (Jackie Kennedy?) to glitter-encrusted disco twigs (Betty Ford?), the range of Yuletide adornments is both staggering and fascinating.

It was in this Aladdin's cave of vintage szhoosh that I came upon a vast quantity of large, shiny plastic balls. Little did I know it when I found them, but these hideous *objets* were going to have a significant impact on my life.

Approximately six inches in diameter, they resembled something that might dangle from the ceiling of a seventies gay bar or a doomed shopping mall. Setting aside the question of why anyone ever saw fit to introduce such a supremely lowbrow, tacky item into the White House, I grabbed them, all eight hundred of them. I was on a mission. A secret mission.

Spring 2009. Desirée Rogers, the glamazon former White House social secretary, called me—are you sitting down?—and asked me to help decorate the White House for the holidays!

Mr. Gay goes to Washington.

I am the First Fag. I am the First Elf.

I felt honored and stunned but not, if I am to be honest, totally surprised. This may sound arrogant, but if not me then who?

With over thirty-five years of holiday decorating at Barneys and elsewhere, I am, *après tout*, one of the most experienced elves in the land. When I run into other elves on the street, they bow or even curtsy. The young, precocious elves try to kiss my magic ring and yank at my scalloped green felt jerkin. Naughty elves!

My accumulated holiday experience and savoir faire did not stop me from being utterly terrified by this fabulous project. The responsibility! The gravitas! The White House! What would happen if I screwed it all up? What would happen if it all turned out looking all horrid and naff?

Meeting Desirée. March 2009.

Why do I feel as if I am standing in a hole? Because the gorgeous and statuesque Desirée Rogers is five feet ten inches tall, that's why.

During lunch, La Rogers pulls a legal pad out of her Vuitton shoulder bag. She reads me notes taken at a meeting with Mrs. Obama (!) the previous day: Reflect. Rejoice. Renew. This mantra will serve as my guiding principle for the first Obama holiday.

It's hard to describe my emotions. I am excited but I also feel a bit like Mia Farrow in the dream sequence from *Rosemary's Baby*. While Satan is shagging her, she writhes about in a state of semiconsciousness. Finally she opens her eyes and screams, "This is no dream. This is really happening!"

In other words, I'm terrified.

During our chat, I suggest that we incorporate some children's art. Desirée agrees and goes on to tell me about the aforementioned warehouse. A lightbulb goes on. Let's combine the kids' art with a recycling moment! Maybe there will be some big gnarly ornaments from some past administration which can be customized, painted and repurposed. Reflect. Rejoice. Renew. Recycle.

I ride the N train back to the glamorous home I share with my adorable, good-looking and successful husband and our dog, that adorable dingleberry factory named Liberace. I am in a daze. My mind is mincing. My pulse is primping.

This is really happening!

Was I thinking about the honor that had been bestowed on me by my adopted country? Was I glowing with patriotism? Was I kvelling with the meaning and gravitas of it all?

Hell no! I was thinking about *la pooblicitay!*

In a matter of moments after meeting with Desirée I had made the transition from fear to fame whore.

In my mind I saw a rampart of flashbulbs and a horde of photographers screaming my name. You are validated. You are fabulous! You have clawed your way to the middle.

A montage of media moments is slot-machining through my imagination.

Me and Matt Lauer touring the White House.

Me on the cover of *People* magazine glue-gunning paper streamers with Malia and Sasha.

Me and Diane Sawyer throwing snowballs on the front lawn and then doing a cozy sit-down where I reflect on my draining-but-life-changing experience as the First Elf.

Me and Barack and Michelle kicking back around a log fire after the kids have gone to bed, enjoying a vat of eggnog, or in my case, pretending to, since there is nothing on earth I find more revolting than eggnog.

Meeting Mrs. Obama. September 2009.

By September, Desirée, myself and the team were ready to unfurl our reflect/rejoice/renew/recycle game plan to Mrs. Obama.*

Why do I feel as if I am standing in a hole again? Because Mrs. Obama is five feet eleven inches tall, that's why.

Warning: the next four paragraphs are devoid of ribald humor and cynicism. The First Elf is having a sincere moment.

The First Lady looks outstanding in a navy blue and apple green dirndl-skirted summer dress with a waist-accentuating Argyle cardigan. She dresses with the chic understatement of a *Mona Lisa Smile* Wellesley gal circa 1950. She bends down, a very long way down, and gives me a hug and thanks me for my hard work. I'm kvelling.

We show her our concept boards and swatches and talk her through the vast and complex proposal of wreaths and trees and garlands, East Wing, West Wing, the Nativity, Residence, Oval Office, etc., etc. She interjects great ideas and keeps us on track. In a lifetime filled with presentation meetings, this was, for me, the easiest and the most pleasurable. Our First Lady has great taste. She is a quick study. She is delightful and cultivated and inhabits her role with grace and intelligence.

Her long-standing interest in style makes the process easy: She likes the "softer, more Romeo Gigli colors." She agrees with

---

* I provided the overarching vision while Kimberly Merlin, a faghagalicious genius, creatively whomped a solid design proposal together with unerring artistic élan, i.e., she did most of the work. Bravo, Kimmy! And also bravo to Sally Armbruster, Desirée's assistant.

my suggestion that we should use "a Lanvin-ish antique-looking glitter" instead of anything too sparkly.

While Mrs. Obama loves the general direction, her most enthusiastic response is reserved for the eight hundred recycled silver balls which are proposed for the monumental Blue Room tree. Together we decide that decoupage, rather than hand painting, is the way to go. Mrs. Obama suggests that we utilize the efforts of not just kids, but people of all ages at community centers around the United States. The theme? Great American monuments.

Before you can say, "Bo, the Portuguese water dog," the silver plastic balls are shipped off by Sally and her interns to diverse organizations in every state. We include a jug of Mod Podge and a directive written by yours truly on the pitfalls and pleasures of decoupage.

This is really happening!

December 2009. Time to make the doughnuts.

The installation of the holiday décor follows close upon the Manolo heels of the Salahi party-crasher debacle. For the first day of work, I toy with showing up at the White House security gate wearing a red sari, or a T-shirt that says, "Who's Sari now?" A great photo op, right?

WRONG! (Oprah baritone.)

Once inside the White House, I detect an entirely different mood. It is immediately clear that all and any foofy, poofy Elf pooblicitay has been nixed. All because of those Salahis.

Horror. Shock. No publicity! No Oprah! No nothing.

The show must go on. I take a deep philosophical breath, grab my trusty glue gun and head to the Blue Room.

Thanks to those idiot Salahis, security is as tight as an elf's butt-hole. All the incoming boxes of pepper berries, hydrangeas and pine garlands are sniffed and prodded. Extra precautions are taken with the eight hundred formerly-hideous-and-now-hopefully-fabulous silver balls. Coming as they have from such a broad spectrum of locations, they represent a complex security challenge. I am itching to take a look at the results. This will be my first encounter with the hundreds of returning orbs. When they are finally released by security and delivered to the Blue Room, I dive into the boxes à la Greg Louganis, or Esther Williams, depending on how old you are.

Wow! I am astounded by what I find.

This is really happening, Rosemary!

The citizens of the United States of America have done a bang-up job. The balls are the perfect mixture of wholesome holiday cheer, patriotism, creative expression and fun. While there is no shortage of Mount Rushmores, Niagara Falls and Grand Canyons, most of the creators took a more small-town route, commemorating local landmarks and institutions. Inhabitants of an Indian reservation fringed and beaded theirs with extraordinary skill. One clever person turned his/hers into a Georgia peach.

So what if there is no publicity for moi! Everything is looking gorgeous, and that's the only thing that matters. Right?

We are on a very tight deadline. The relentless schedule of White House holiday events starts the next day. While Kimberly and her team fling grapevines, magnolia wreaths and lotus pods hither and thither, I set about the task of festooning the massive, ceiling-scraping Blue Room tree. After eight hours of ball tying, scaffold wrangling, and ribbon pinking, we are done. On Wednesday, December 2, we add the magnificent hand-beaded Project Alabama tree skirt. *Et voilà!* I am very proud of our "Monuments" tree. It looks gorgeous.

A pang of sadness.

This would be the perfect moment for the sit-down with Katie Couric. The press blackout is once more starting to rattle my gay cage. All this work and szhoosh and festooning, but what does it all mean unless Jeanne Moos is there from CNN chatting with me as I dangle the final dingle.

Where is my pooblicitay?

Hearing a racket outside I turn and manage to catch sight of President Obama jumping aboard the Marine 1 helicopter to go make his now-famous West Point Afghanistan speech. This was the final nail in the First Elf's publicity coffin. Finally, I was forced to acknowledge that there might, just might, be more important stuff going on in the world than my need for a pink follow-spot and a four-page how-I-did-it editorial in *Vanity Fair.*

On my way back to the szhooshy W Hotel across the street, I reflect on the majesty of the United States: A gay elf can immigrate to this country with a dollar and a dream and, if he schleps hard enough, end up szhooshing the White House. Publicity, schmublicity. Salahi, schmalahi! I was happy to have donated my time and creativity to my adopted homeland, and to the first black president of the United States. I needed no external validation.

Maybe one day, I muse as I slide into the crisp hotel sheets after chewing ravenously through a lesbian nut concoction which was the only thing I could find to eat in the minibar, there will be a gay prezzie . . .

During the first three weeks of December the White House schedule of fetes and receptions proceeds without incident. Nothing collapses. Everyone is happy. Even Pat Nixon's old, embellished Fabergé orbs, polished up and reused in one of many bipartisan gestures, are happy.

December 23.

The diminutive attention junkie finally gets his external validation fix.

Some horrid little camera-phone snaps of my Blue Room tree find their way onto an archconservative website.

The images in question contain carefully chosen and gruesomely misleading micro close-ups of three of the eight hundred decoupaged Blue Room balls.

The first image is of a barely visible postage-stamp-size Andy Warhol's Chairman Mao from, I assume, a Pittsburgh Warhol Museum–themed ball. (Andy, a fellow window-dressing attention junkie, was born in Pittsburgh.)

Next comes a micro mug shot of the good-hearted vaudevillian drag queen entertainer known as Hedda Lettuce.

And last but not least, guess who? A pecan-size Obama head, superimposed by a fan onto the Mount Rushmore presidential lineup.

These three details are seized upon and attributed directly to yours truly. The headline on the website screams out: TRANSVESTITES, MAO AND OBAMA ORNAMENTS DECORATE WHITE HOUSE TREE.

The posting implies that I, Simon Doonan, the First Elf, have manipulated the content of the White House décor to incorporate my own malevolent gay agenda, express Communist sympathies and launch an attack on family values by including a mug shot of Hedda Lettuce.

All hell breaks loose.

There is no way to even begin to address the idiocy and inaccuracy of these notions. There is no such thing as *redress* on the curse that we call the Internet. I have been well and truly dropped in the shazzit and the homophobic hating begins.

This is no dream. This is really happening!

Within hours Hedda and mini-Mao have gone viral and global. Fox News rants. There are tens of thousands of blogs and hits and twits and twats. Homicidal invective rages. Even Gawker fanned the flames, calling me a "noted gay male." How about "ping-pong ace" or "animal lover" or "former aerobics whiz" or "world's oldest window dresser" or "third-rate hooker" or "a noted Chinchilla"?

There are many other facets to the First Elf, you know.

My website starts receiving death threats involving baseball bats and my head, etc. You get the picture.

Be careful what you wish for . . .

I e-mail my White House contact and ask them what to do.

Buy a helmet.

Merry Christmas, Mr. Doonan, and welcome to Tinselgate.

As somebody who was raised by a Tory working-class mom and a lefty dad, I am no stranger to the concept of a feisty debate. But why the threats of violence? The willingness of wing-nut Web devotees everywhere to jump aboard the hostility train was staggering and extremely unfestive. The one person who kept her sense of humor was Hedda Lettuce herself. (She had apparently decorated her particular orb while volunteering at a senior gay fund-raiser.) Spewing double entendres, she blogged about the exhilaration she experienced knowing that one of her balls was now hanging on the White House tree.

The irony of the story: Finally, I had my attention junkie impulses under control. I had squished my need for external validation and crammed it, metaphorically, into a tiny evening clutch and stuffed it in a drawer. I had made peace with the fact that there would be no publicity when—wham!—I got far more than any fame whore could ever have wanted.

The moral of the story: Don't sit at home clutching your pearls in the dark. Whenever possible, you must decoupage your balls and dangle them in public view. However, when the reviews come out, try really, really hard not to read the comments page.

Bonne chance!

About the Author

Simon Doonan is the author of *Eccentric Glamour* and *Wacky Chicks* as well as the memoirs *Confessions of a Window Dresser* and *Nasty*, which was adapted for television under the title *Beautiful People*. Originally from England, he worked on Savile Row and elsewhere before becoming the long-time creative director for Barneys New York, where he created legendary window displays for more than twenty years. Formerly a columnist for *The New York Observer*, he now writes a biweekly column for *Slate* and has appeared on countless national TV shows, including *Gossip Girl*, the *I Love the* series, *Iron Chef America*, and *America's Next Top Model*, as a commentator and contributor on all things stylish. Doonan lives in New York City with his husband, Jonathan Adler.

1-12